WATER FEATURES FOR SMALL GARDENS

WATER FEATURES FOR SMALL GARDENS

FRANCESCA GREENOAK

Trafalgar Square Publishing

First published in the United States of America in 1996 by
Trafalgar Square Publishing
North Pomfret
Vermont 05053

Printed and bound in Hong Kong

First published in Great Britain in 1996 by
Conran Octopus Limited
37 Shelton Street
London WC2H 9HN

Commissioning Editor: Sarah Pearce
Project Editor: Caroline Davidson
American Editor: Marjorie Dietz
Art Editor: Tony Seddon
Picture Research: Jessica Walton
Production: Mano Mylvaganam
Illustrator: Antonia Enthoven
Index: Atha Bellman Associates

Library of Congress Catalog Card Number:
95-62177

ISBN 1-57076-053-5

Produced by Mandarin Offset

CONTENTS

INTRODUCTION

No activity in the world is as therapeutic as watching water, whether this is the natural surge of the sea, the gentle spluttering of a stream or the reflective stillness of a pool. These are qualities that we also find desirable in our gardens, especially in a locality unblessed with rivers or streams. I can think of no single item that has given me greater pleasure in my small cottage garden than the pond with its irises, water lilies and wild flowers and its simple frog spout. The experience of my own pool made me look curiously at how others managed to bring water into their gardens and I have come to think that, in many ways, I prefer the artistry and ingenuity of small water gardens to those more suited to larger landscapes. I also discovered how easy, as well as satisfying, it is to introduce water into a small garden.

LEFT Water spouts from a lion's head mask mounted on a leafy town wall splashing over cobbles piled up in a algae-covered sink. Golden hop *Humulus lupulus* 'Aureus' brightens the shaded wall, contrasting with the neatly clipped box plants placed in front of the sink.

ABOVE This small rock-edged pool has an all-season planting of dwarf conifers and cotoneaster (*Cotoneaster microphyllus*). Smooth pebbles contrast with the rough-cut rock and the overall effect is brightened by the variegated foliage of ivy, iris and hosta, while small water lilies sprinkle the surface of the water.

This book investigates the art of bringing water into a confined space in ways that reflect the personality of the gardener and match the style of planting in the garden and the architecture of the house. In the course of my research I have been struck by the effect that can be produced by even the simplest artefact if it is skilfully placed. A bowl filled with water, for example, can create a bold focus when set in a prominent position or on a raised support. Placed in a quiet corner of the garden, it gives rise to ideas for plant associations, such as ferns with sweet woodruff (*Galium odoratum*) and lily-of-the-valley (*Convallaria majalis*), that will create a special microclimate.

As so much water life is naturally small-scale, there should be no difficulty in finding plants to suit tiny pools. Azolla is a minuscule aquatic plant, whose small lacy leaves are gray-green or bright green in the spring and summer, turning to red and deep brown later in the year as the cold begins to bite. Like the less decorative but hardier duckweed, the floating aquatic, azolla, gently shades the water from extremes of heat. There are also attractive pond weeds and other plants, such as water lilies and the fragrant water hawthorn (*Aponogeton distachyos*), which, rooted in deeper water, will rise to the surface to produce floating flowers and leaves. If a pool is not deep enough to hold plants, there are many marginal plants, notably ferns and irises, hostas and astilbes, which flourish in the humidity of the surrounding area.

There is an astonishing variety of ways in which even the less experienced gardener can introduce water into a small area, ranging from a simple pond to a commissioned water sculpture. A pond can be naturalistic – planted with wild flowers such as yellow flag iris (*Iris pseudacorus*), water mint (*Mentha aquatica*), lady's smock (*Cardamine pratensis*), and snake's-head fritillary (*Fritillaria meleagris*). By using exotic garden cultivars, you achieve a more ornamental look that can be either flowery, reflective and formal, or leafy, green and mysterious.

Bird baths, bowls, copper containers, sinks, troughs and wooden barrels provide variations on a different theme. Gravel, pebbles and rocks can be reinterpreted in numerous ways, as can the diverse kinds of jet and fountain. Perhaps the most economical use of space is a wall-mounted fountain seen in many gardens, but here again, the personal inventiveness of each gardener results in a wide variety of interpretations of this basic idea.

Introducing water into the garden brings with it a range of possibilities for the surrounding plants. This book places a strong emphasis on the plant preferences of each gardener, which in each case determine the individuality of the overall effect. It is the dynamic interaction between artefact, form and water that

ABOVE A tiny pool tucked in between the slate paving slabs of a small courtyard that is crammed with plants. The foliage of the golden hop (*Humulus lupulus* 'Aureus') and variegated fatsia (*Fatsia japonica* 'Variegata') is intertwined with the pink flowers of roses, clematis and fuchsia. Pots of agapanthus, violas and pelagoniums surround the pool.

creates a special impression. Using water in gardens becomes exciting when it is not simply a matter of placing the pool, fountain or waterfall in the best spot, but also of managing the light and shade, color and texture of the growing plants. No water feature looks the same two seasons running. This is particularly appropriate for small gardens which require more variation than most so that the eye does not tire of the same confined vista, however beautiful.

Water animates the whole garden even if it fits into only a tiny part. I was very much struck on my first visit to the exquisite garden at the Museum of Garden History, situated next to the Archbishop's Palace in one of the busiest parts of London, by the way in which the light splash of the wall fountain distracted the ear from the appalling roar of traffic just beyond the hedge.

Small gardens are on the increase world-wide, especially in towns where the designs tend to be inward-looking, places of calm and restoration, with planting designed to screen out ugly intrusions from the outside world. In such gardens water can have a special significance. Indeed, there are therapists who use the rhythms and sounds of water as a means of soothing and replenishing the spirit. Water sculptures can be seen in gardens, atria and public places all over the world but there are also smaller versions for use in private gardens. They work on the

principle that the shape of the sculpture sets up vortices which, in turn, create a rhythmic flow in the water. Interestingly, this seems to have a beneficial effect upon plants and fish as well as people.

No expanse of water seems so insignificant that it cannot be alluring. Even a small surface will reflect the clouds and surrounding trees and plants, and attract birds and insects. I have seen a dragonfly investigating a minute pond, and frogs in a pool almost as small, and watched bluetits carrying nesting materials into a recessed pipe no longer needed as an overflow during a warm, dry spring. The first animals, usually dainty pond skaters who flit over the surface of the pool, sometimes arrive within hours of a pond being filled for the first time. Later, there will be other visitors such as newts, toads, beetles and small ram's-horn snails. These are the creatures that, together with aquatic plants, help to maintain the natural balance of the pool.

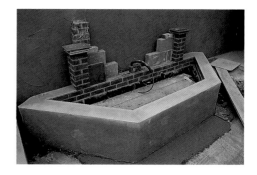

Some sculptors and landscape designers specialize in using water in their work. William Pye, known internationally for his large pieces of sculpture, also provides small-scale designs especially for private gardens. Exhibitions of garden art reveal all kinds of shapes and innovations as well as the more traditional bowls, pots, bird baths and waterfalls, which can make a welcome alternative to conventional mermaids and cherubs.

While some of the water features in this

book are the work of artists or garden designers, most were created by everyday gardeners who found original ways of introducing water, often into the most unpropitious of spaces. Amongst these skilful amateurs were some who, having brought the element of water into their garden, went on to develop other ideas, such as juxtaposing still water with small fountains and falls. It was interesting to find that visitors asked more questions about the water feature than the plants in even the most beautifully planted gardens.

I hope this book will demonstrate not only the beauty of water and the variety of ways in which it can be incorporated into small gardens but also how easy this is to do in practice.

ABOVE A close-up of the finished wall-mounted fountain and pebble pool. Water from the Neptune head pours over the pebbles, which rest on a grid of metal mesh specially made to fit by the local blacksmith. The plants on either side are Egyptian paper rushes (*Cyperus papyrus*).

OPPOSITE PAGE A sequence of pictures showing some of the stages in creating this pool. The unruly ivy and pyracantha were stripped off the wall and the ornamental bricks on the top of the wall were removed. The wall was built up again with standard bricks, roughly rendered and painted with sandy-colored matt emulsion. The foundations of the pond were dug, triangular shelving built into each side, the raised sides were built up in breeze block, and then a brick arch was added over the pool. A butyl liner was laid in the pool, smoothed down and two courses of brick were added on top.

A protective pipe was inserted into the brick course and the electric cable from the transformer was connected to the electric pump at the bottom of the pool and to the two pool lights which were recessed into the front of the basin. The water pipe from the pump was also taken through the brick course and set into the wall which was finally smooth-rendered and painted.

ROCKY POOLS AND PEBBLE FEATURES

Water shining on pebbles brings out the grain of the stone and the beauty of the imperfections: speckled gray-white crystals in granite, a vein of marble or quartzite, or a red or green-tinged slate. There are few who can resist picking up a gleaming stone from a newly washed shingle beach or a stony lakeside. The same glistening effect can be recreated in a garden by arranging pebbles in the basin of a fountain. Gray, red and white colors can then be chosen to contrast with or reflect the stone, brick or painted woodwork of the house. The fountain itself, whether it is a dancing spray, an umbrella fountain or a simple jet, can also be used to reflect a certain mood or feeling.

LEFT A bold gushing spout of water crashes down on to a cairn of large ammonites, and thence to a rocky pool surrounded by mostly hardy grasses, irises, ivies and the imposing royal fern (*Osmunda regalis*).

ABOVE Rocks, slabs and crazy paving are alleviated in this gray and green and blue composition by a discreet lining of attractive blue and white tiles around the circular pool. This is an all-season, all day and night garden with evergreens and dainty lighting which brings the scene to life at night with splashing water, gleaming tiles and wet rock, and shadows thrown by the plants. Note that the rocks that make the spills stand out to create a gush rather than a trickle.

There is a relaxed formality about pebble pools that makes them ideal for small gardens. Their distinctive qualities reward a close attention to siting, whether this is near a door or window, or a place where you customarily sit outdoors. Also, because they generally hug the ground, rock and pebble pools are best positioned where they can accentuate a point between beds or borders, or on a level space on one side of a path, rather than as the focal point of a vista, unless you can place it on rising ground.

Many people like big, gray cobbles; others prefer a mixture of colors. Variety is important in a small garden, so it is worth considering different ideas. Some stones have a naturally greenish or reddish tint which could complement or contrast with the color of garden furniture, paving or the paintwork of the house. Water garden specialists and some garden centers can supply different kinds or advise on sources. In a small pool, shells could also be employed with, or instead of, the pebbles. Large, rosy-colored cockle shells, for example, which you may find in a seafood market, look beautiful either on their own or with pebbles. Try to vary the style of the pebbles or the surrounding plants when you begin to tire of your initial project. This makes for a refreshing change without you having to resort to a complete redesign.

The margin of the pebble pool can be defined formally by dwarf box (*Buxus sempervirens* 'Suffruticosa') or attractive trailing plants such as Creeping Jenny (*Lysimachia nummularia*) or ferns, or edged with brick or paving. For larger rocky pools, it is necessary to excavate and line the pool with a flexible liner (*see p. 54*) or, alternatively, use a large container such as an old water tank as the reservoir to supply the fountain. Lay heavy duty mesh over this and cut out a square through which you can reach to prime the pump, clean the filter and clear the bottom of silt. Put a larger piece of mesh over the square which you can remove easily when you need to carry out any of these operations.

I have seen pebble pools made more eye-catching in raised containers: a stone trough, for example, looks striking with pebbles heaped inside it. The pump, in this case, would be positioned inside the container or, preferably, in a reservoir in the ground beneath. A terracotta container or a wooden barrel could also be used and filled with smaller-grade pebbles, which you could have already polished.

Another option is to rehabilitate a formal pool by lining it with a layer of pebbles, thus converting it into a pebble pool. Keep the pebbles just covered with water so that you can see their colors. Lining a circular, concrete pool with a mortar mixture, cobbled Portuguese-style with close-fitting pebbles, and placing a small fountain in the center, is another attractive variation on this theme.

ABOVE Small drips from the fish leak back into the soil and dampen the ferns: soft shield (*Polystichum setiferum*), American maidenhair (*Adiantum pedatum*) and hart's-tongue (*Asplenium scolopendrium*). The variegated shrub behind is the unusual semi-hardy *Pittosporum tenuifolium* 'Irene Patterson', which has undulating evergreen leaves. Beside the pebble pool are *Houttuynia cordata* and *H.* 'Chameleon', and the dainty maple, *Acer palmatum* var. *dissectum*.

ABOVE This design uses an attractive rock, gneiss banded with quartzite, which has been drilled so that a water spout can be fed through it to flow over the irregular grains and lines. The pompons of the polygonum (*Persicaria bistorta* 'Superba', syn. *Polygonum bistorta*), the dainty blades of *Carex morrowii* 'Evergold' and *Spiraea japonica* 'Goldflame' enhance the effect.

A ground-level pebble pool can go down to very small size, about 30cm (12in) in diameter for a circular shape, but slightly more space should be allowed if you want a liner, extending beyond the edge, to catch the drips and drain them back. A good way to construct the pool is to dig a hole to contain a small reservoir (a trash can or plastic flower bucket will do nicely) beneath the spot where it is to be sited. Place a small pump in the tank, resting on a brick to avoid any silt that collects on the bottom being sucked into it.

Cut a circle of wire mesh 12cm (5in) wider than the proposed pool size and place it over the reservoir and anchor it into the soil with wire bent to form staples. You can lay a ring of liner the same size under the wire mesh if you are anxious to recycle all of the water, but if you make sure the reservoir is always kept pretty full by topping it up when you water the garden a liner will not be necessary. Pebbleside plants will benefit from being able to root more deeply and from the extra spray. Whatever you do, wind and evaporation always cause a certain amount of water loss, so regular topping up is important.

When the reservoir and mesh are satisfactorily in place, with the spout for the jet slightly protruding, begin to lay on the pebbles, working from the outside inwards. The pump should be adjusted to a low spray that reaches almost to the edge of the pebble circle on a windless day.

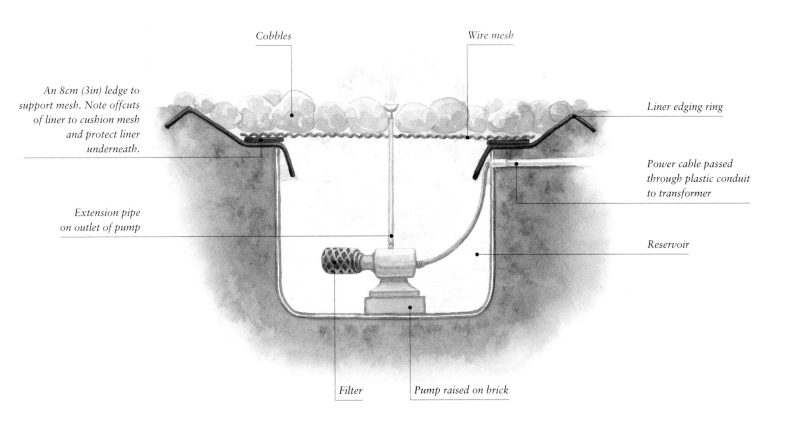

Cobbles

Wire mesh

An 8cm (3in) ledge to support mesh. Note offcuts of liner to cushion mesh and protect liner underneath.

Liner edging ring

Power cable passed through plastic conduit to transformer

Extension pipe on outlet of pump

Reservoir

Filter

Pump raised on brick

For larger, shallow, pebble-lined pools, the best method is to use a liner (*see p.54*) and to line it carefully with shingle, pebbles or rocks, or combinations of different forms of rock. When planting pools of this kind, you must remember that marginal plants need pockets of soil or to be planted at the edge of the liner so that they can get their roots down. You could also try planting up pots, which can then be disguised by the pebbles. Trailing plants can also be encouraged to grow down towards the water's edge.

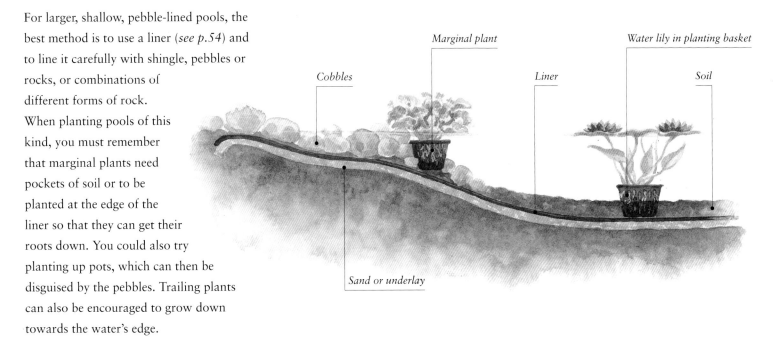

Marginal plant

Water lily in planting basket

Cobbles

Liner

Soil

Sand or underlay

LEFT The dominant brushstrokes in this still pool are in green and white: the abundant foliage of the polygonum, glossy water lily pads, bergenia and marsh marigold provide contrast for white nicotiana, water lilies and water poppies, the bronze-leaved lobelia (*Lobelia cardinalis*), and the annual Mexican daisies (*Erigeron karvinskianus*) with their charming pink and off-white flowers. Note the way the purple smudges on the lily pads are brought out by the purple foliage of lobelia – *Lobelia* x *gerardii* 'Vedrariensis' is a very good color – and how the gold of the pitcher plant (*Sarracenia purpurea*) finds echoes in the golds of the foliage.

RIGHT A magical rocky pool with the foliage greens lit up by the yellow single roses and variegated leaves. This planting includes ferns such as the easily grown male fern (*Dryopteris filix-mas*), an equally easily pleased, velvet-leaved lady's mantle (*Alchemilla mollis* or *A. erythropoda*), gold-variegated ivy (*Hedera helix* 'Buttercup'), a spreading golden rose such as 'Canary Bird' and a gold-splashed elaeagnus (*Elaeagnus* x *ebbingei* 'Gilt Edge') and yellow violas.

ABOVE An artificial streamlet almost hidden among the hummocks of pink
and lilac plants in a nicely-aged, moss-covered rockery. Rock plants come in all
shapes and colors, but here the owner has kept to this color scheme for
summer: hardy geraniums, scented pinks (*Dianthus*) and thymes from the
Mediterranean with their green and gray-green foliage.

RIGHT An attractive bright effect has been created
by using yellow-colored rock and stone chippings
of the same shade, contrasting with gray pebbles.
The planting around a pool like this should tone
with the stone colors, as do the golden deadnettle
(*Lamium maculatum* 'Aureum') and gray-green
lady's mantle (*Alchemilla mollis*), which captures
the dewdrops and rain on its foliage. The gray
stones are set off by *Heuchera micrantha* var.
diversifolia 'Palace Purple' and lifted by the pink
flowers of the feathery astilbes and bottle-brush
head of the polygonum (*Persicaria macrophylla*).

ABOVE Here the dominant effect is confined to gold and gray against a background of green foliage. The small pool reflects the brilliant yellow of the flag (*Iris pseudacorus*) with its spear-like leaves. There are several yellow sedums which create a golden ground-hugging effect; among the best is *Sedum kamtschaticum* var. *floriferum* 'Weihenstephaner Gold', but the common rockery *Sedum acre*, though not as dense, will also give a pretty effect.

ABOVE An unusual waterfall, with water gushing over and through a pile of rocks and pebbles, is overhung by bamboo foliage to create a moody oriental effect of light and shade and contrasting textures. A hardy bamboo for smaller gardens is *Pleioblastus auricomus* which takes on beautiful golden-green variegations when grown in full sun. The sedge (*Carex morrowii* 'Evergold') is another suitable plant that would create the same color effect.

THE CROSSING HOUSE

This small garden is hidden away in an English village. Situated next to a railway line, it has become a honeypot for garden enthusiasts who appreciate the distinctiveness and variety of the planting and design. It is, however, the imaginative use of water that prompts most questions from visitors. Coaxing ingenuity to the limits, the owners have introduced water, in different forms, to six different places in the garden.

The crowning delight of the garden is the circular pebble pool, which is surrounded by a mini-hedge of dwarf box. It is a design that draws the eye, becoming an effective focal point when viewed from any place in the garden. Close to, it reveals an unsuspected dimension because the wet pebbles are quite beautiful in themselves. Many contain ammonite and trilobite fossils. The owners and their family have gradually collected unusual rock types over the years and they know each rock individually. The gentle spray from a central spout keeps them glistening like newly washed shingle on a beach.

Complementing the pebble circle is a tiny pond made from an old laundry copper, which is in effect a large copper bucket, with plants grouped gracefully around it. There are two more copper ponds where the garden extends on the other side of the house and a diminutive, tiered fountain in a shady corner on the opposite side. In addition, there is a small waterfall, trickling over imported rock to a small but deep pool, which is itself connected beneath the path to a larger pool edged by the lawn on one side and a rocky hummock on the other.

ABOVE This box circle is formed by the small-leaved cultivar (*Buxus sempervirens* 'Suffruticosa'). The hedging, which is continued along the path, and the neat box spiral help to hold the elements of the design together.

House

Copper pond

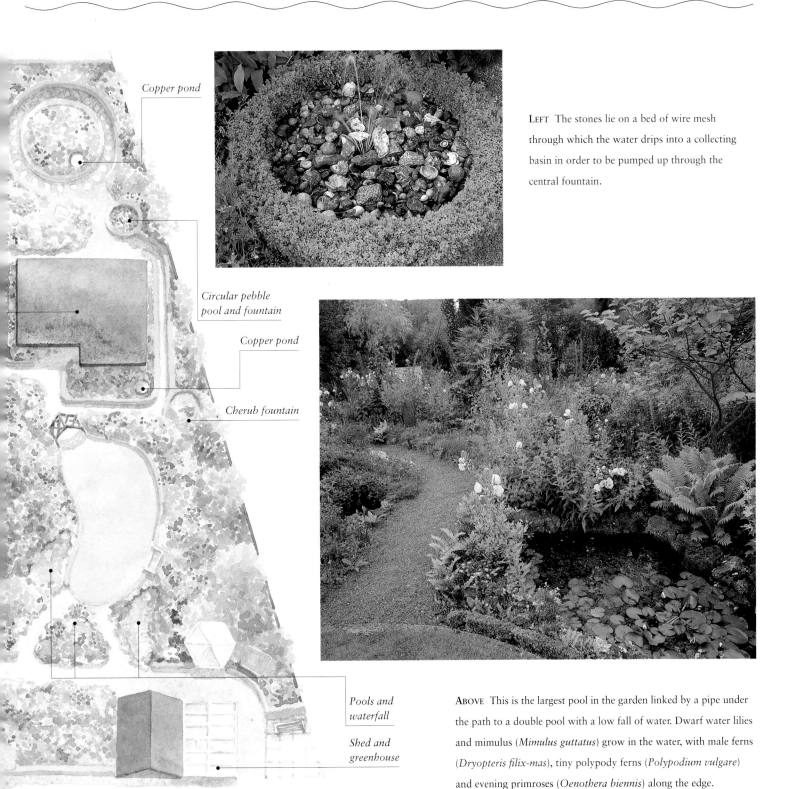

Copper pond

Circular pebble
pool and fountain

Copper pond

Cherub fountain

Pools and
waterfall

Shed and
greenhouse

LEFT The stones lie on a bed of wire mesh through which the water drips into a collecting basin in order to be pumped up through the central fountain.

ABOVE This is the largest pool in the garden linked by a pipe under the path to a double pool with a low fall of water. Dwarf water lilies and mimulus (*Mimulus guttatus*) grow in the water, with male ferns (*Dryopteris filix-mas*), tiny polypody ferns (*Polypodium vulgare*) and evening primroses (*Oenothera biennis*) along the edge.

FORMAL PONDS AND SPLASH FOUNTAINS

Formal ponds and fountains have been popular ornaments in small, enclosed gardens from the Middle Ages onwards. Formal ponds create a sense of stillness and order and, positioned cleverly, they can also give an illusion of greater space. They can be easily adapted to any style of garden, whether this is a naturalistic garden full of wild flowers or a more formal garden. Fountains that create a splash or bubble are invaluable, not only for their visual effect, but for the soothing sound of water that they bring into the garden. The sight and sound of water rising and falling back into a pool will make an appealing contribution to an otherwise serene garden.

LEFT Cottage garden plants growing attractively in and through crazy paving create an informal effect in an urban situation. The split jets of water rise as high as the white campanulas. The pool is protected from autumn leaves by a net stretched from the metal runners neatly set around the inner edge.

A formal pool can be enhanced by means of neat, narrow hedging, raised up to about 30cm (12in). The hedge can be made of dwarf box, lavender or cotton lavender (*Santolina chamaecyparissus*), depending on whether you prefer a rich evergreen or a scented gray. Pools that are raised to 60cm (2ft) or more, and faced with a material such as stone or brick, are best left as informal sitting places, decorated simply with an arrangement of plants in a variety of pots and containers.

Formal pools that are level with the ground work well on a small scale. A dark panel of water in a paved or bricked area adds an element to the garden unmatched by any other. The tiniest formal pools are best kept simple in shape, without embellishment or movement. For those larger than 90cm (3ft) each way, consider which shape best suits the style and proportions of your garden.

Large pools can be embellished with the graceful arcs and sounds of fountains set within the pool or splashing from the edge. In earlier times, they involved complicated hydraulics but modern domestic pumps mean amateurs can install them in even the smallest of garden spaces.

Pools with fountains work best if they are disciplined by a degree of formality. Fountain jets, sited on a poolside of brick or stone, can be supported by grouped pots as well as small neat beds of flowers and foliage. The shape of the fountain can be echoed by the surrounding planting.

ABOVE A most unusual centerpiece recalls the flowery meadows of the Middle Ages on the tiniest possible scale. The ornamental metal pot is edged with turf planted with daisies and buttercups. Water splashes from the central spout onto a mosaic roundel glimpsed through a veil of golden leaf blades. The hardy *Carex elata* 'Aurea' is a beautiful sedge for a pool or bog garden; another is *Carex morrowii* 'Evergold'. A number of ornamental daisies could be used in this scheme.

The arching foliage of plants such as hostas, irises, astilbes and ferns is especially effective. Roses that have a compact, rounded habit also look lovely by the margins of a pool. *Rosa* 'Raubritter' is a classic rose with full-petalled, dark pink blooms but is barely scented and tends to mildew later in the season; *R.* 'De Rescht' is a lovely, rich carmine-colored Portland rose, which makes a neat fragrant mound; *R.* 'Baby Love', a new yellow rose, is both scented and compact.

Most fountains come with attachments for various kinds of jet so that you can have differently shaped fountain heads. Although it is best not to go for an arrangement that is overly complicated in a small pool, it is still possible to vary the arc of a single jet, a split jet, or three, five or multiple small-thread jets to provide a change of pace. This can be welcome within a small space.

Frog or toad fountains, which are perhaps more suitable for informal or wildlife pools, also look attractive set in a semi-natural way amongst poolside plants, though you have to be careful that they do not get overwhelmed by plant growth. Plants grow but the fountain is fixed, so always bring your outlet connecting pipe out a little further beyond the foliage than you think necessary. It is also a good idea to keep the distance that the piping has to run as short as possible in order to reduce the strain on the pump.

LEFT No attempt is made to make the planting look natural in this rectangular raised pond. Pots of shade-tolerant plants are almost submerged and covered with decorative pebbles to keep their compost in place. Growing gunnera (*Gunnera magellanica*) in a pot is a good way to keep this giant in order and the cyperus sedges such as Nile grass (*Cyperus involucratus*), with their Egyptian-style starry leafbracts, are among the daintiest plants for the water garden.

BELOW The fountain-sculpture makes a good centerpiece for this semi-formal pool with its cobbled edging. The geometry of the paving and design is offset by the abundant planting of variegated flags (*Iris pseudacorus* 'Variegata') in the pond and large shrubs in the surrounding beds. Pots of variegated cordyline, lilies and agapanthus with their distinctive foliage and colors can be rearranged to create variety.

When constructing a formal pond the area should be excavated as accurately and cleanly as possible as a poorly dug and lined pool may result in unstable and crumbling sides. For maximum strength, dig the pool sides at least 10 degrees off the vertical. Put down an underlay of protective carpet or geo-textile matting.

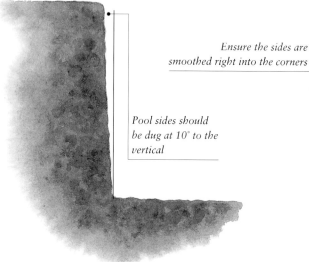

Ensure the sides are smoothed right into the corners

Pool sides should be dug at 10° to the vertical

Bricks placed strategically will hold the liner in place while it is being fitted; take care not to damage the liner

To measure the butyl or PVC liner needed take the length of the pond plus twice the maximum depth, and the width of the pond plus twice the maximum depth; add a final 30cm (12in) for folding and fitting. Put the liner in the center of the pond and smooth the base flat. Next ease the liner into the corners. Smooth the sides flat, using bricks to weight the liner in place, then create a large flap from the surplus at each corner. Fold this over neatly. Fill the pond with water to take up any slack and then cut the flap above the waterline and tuck the material over for a neat fit.

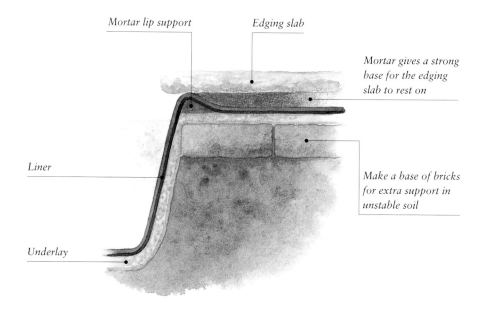

Mortar lip support

Edging slab

Mortar gives a strong base for the edging slab to rest on

Liner

Make a base of bricks for extra support in unstable soil

Underlay

When a formal pool is surrounded by paving, the slabs may be taken slightly over the pool edge, making an attractive finish. Remove the topsoil down to water level, then, if your soil is light, remove a further 10cm (4in) of soil and replace this with bricks to provide a firm base. Bring your underlay up over the bricks, then place a line of mortar around the pool edge; this will raise the liner up to slab height and also seal it to the ground. Now bring the liner up and over this lip, and cover it with a layer of mortar up to the height of the raised edge. Lay your slabs on top, pressing them down securely.

Fountains are amongst the simplest water displays to install as well as one of the most effective and prettiest ways of using water in the smaller garden. Use a submersible pump, positioned at the bottom of the pool with its outlet spout pointing upwards to connect with the fountain unit. Both pump and fountain unit should be supported on a raised flat surface, such as a brick, to keep them clear of the detritus that collects at the bottom of a pool. It is safest to run the power cable from the pool through a plastic conduit under a slab, before burying it in the ground.

ABOVE The simplicity of this garden is a matter of studied effect rather than accident: the stillness of the pool, with the low box-hedging surround, contrasts with the slightly overgrown hedge and the single roses. The bright color of the golden irises stands out against the shade, while their spiky leaves contrast well with the water lily pads and show up the flatness of the brick edges and the enclosing box.

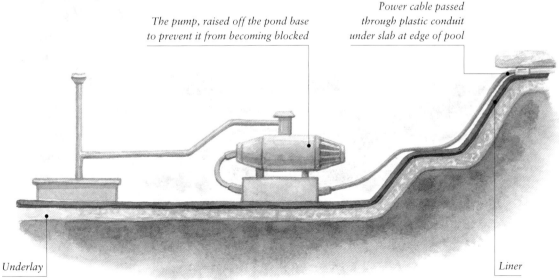

The pump, raised off the pond base to prevent it from becoming blocked

Power cable passed through plastic conduit under slab at edge of pool

Underlay

Liner

LEFT The glorious muddle of planting around this small raised brick pond with its resting stone lion focuses attention on the cool dark water. The warm pinky-red of the tall hybrid tea rose is echoed by the verbenas on the further bank, and the paler pinks of the penstemons and hardy geraniums blend in with the colors of the brick. The variegated *Pittosporum tenuifolium* 'Silver Queen' and the gardener's garters grass (*Phalaris arundinacea* 'Picta') provide contrast and light, while the purple foliage of *Lobelia cardinalis* blends darkly into the water undisturbed by the small spout contained in its cockle-shell.

BELOW A crazy paving edge to this raised pond matches the blue-pink of the surrounding brick paving. Simplicity is the key, with a lone white water lily flower dazzling against its dark foliage. Water lilies do not like moving water but the gentle spill from the poolside frog creates a few bubbles but no serious disturbance. For a pool about 1m (39in) in diameter consider the easily grown hardy (zone-3-11) white water lily *Nymphaea* 'Walter Pagels' or *N*. 'Marliacea Albida' which has darker leaves. You will need a depth of about 20-60cm (8in-2ft), which makes them very suitable for a small raised pool.

ABOVE The water lilies in this brightly lit semi-circular raised pool contend for attention with the brilliant shiny mosaic decoration of the poolside. The soft orange-brown bricks match the terracotta tiling surrounding the pool. This is a design for a hot spot with colors that can take on the glare of the sun.

RIGHT An unusual wooden edging, aged to gray, gives this pool a link with the gray cobble paving. Its slightly irregular shape gives it an extra focus, as well as providing a nook for the *Pontederia cordata,* while the spidery water soldier (*Stratiotes aloides*) dominates the main rectangle. Around it the informal planting provides a range of contrasts in greens and golden foliage including the lesser periwinkle (*Vinca minor* 'Variegata'), lady's mantle (*Alchemilla mollis*), astilbe, clumps of violets, bamboo and the male fern (*Dryopteris filix-mas*).

LEFT A gap between paving has been designed to provide a small pane of water animated by the tiniest of bubble fountains. Roses spill over the surrounding plants and petals float among the tiny lily leaves and purple-leaved *Lobelia cardinalis*. The different colors, textures and shapes of the surrounding plants are brought together to a certain extent by the focus of the pool.

LEFT Three joyful frogs joined together to celebrate six high waterspouts make an irresistibly cheerful piece of sculpture. The spouts are complemented by the spearlike leaves of variegated yellow flag (*Iris pseudacorus* 'Variegata'), phormium and tall arching grass.

ABOVE A sparkling display from minijets of water set around the periphery of a circular brick-edged pool, itself the center point of a pergola swathed with wisteria which casts dappled shade. The box hedging at the base of the pergola creates a neat crisp edge to the flowerbeds and complements the brick edging of the pool.

BELOW A lovely mock-shell made in aqueous glass lying in a bed of wet pebbles. The shapes, colors and textures of the ferns and saxifrage, and the grays of the stone make a simple but effective context for this piece of water sculpture, setting it off perfectly.

ABOVE (LEFT TO RIGHT) Single stage high, three stage, bell jet, single stage low and parasol fountain heads.

THE ASP FOUNTAIN

This sunken area was designed to fit into a sun-baked garden in a rain forest region in Australia, but its ideas can be adapted to suit hot spots in temperate climates. The central fountain is fixed in a bright octagon of sandstone crazy paving, just over 90cm (3ft) across. Raised up to about 30cm (12in), the fountain is faced with bold tiling and encircled with clumps of violets. The spout is composed of two hollow metal pipes fashioned into the form of snakes and gracefully intertwined so that the two heads spout in opposite directions.

Creating shade was a priority in this garden and the designer, Phillip O'Malley, has provided a canopy of tall palms. Surrounding the crazy paving is a square of tropical planting, including cordyline, coffee, macadamia and acacia. Some of these names are familiar all over the world, while others are more local. Many of the plants produce edible fruit which is an added pleasure for the owners, who can use their garden for entertaining a few friends seated on the bench, or a larger party on the paved area.

ABOVE A stepped path on the right leads into the sunken garden where a rustic stone bench has been built into the dry wall. The six pillars of red stone, which are regularly spaced around the outside of the paved area, are used to support large, outdoor candles.

RIGHT A detail of this pool showing the texture of the concrete smoothed into a rounded ridge and the tiles set into the side. Wisely, since the tiles are detailed, the designer has kept the plant surround simple. The glossy leaves nicely echo the reflective water surface. There are over 500 different kinds of violet and it is possible in most countries to find one that suits the situation and climate.

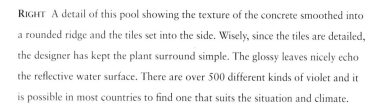

Stepping ston

Mixture of local rainforest
trees and shrubs

Stone bench

Palms

The asp fountain

Steps

Palms

ABOVE This close-up of the fountain shows the intertwined asps, each with a bifurcated spout (in emulation of the snake's forked tongue).

ABOVE The view of the patio and fountain looking from the steps: the bench is taken away when a party is held in the garden to make more room.

Bowls and Tubs

The simplest ideas for introducing water into the garden are often the most effective. You do not need anything more sophisticated than a container whose shape suits the style of your garden. You could, for example, fill an elegant bowl for birds to drink from or bathe in, or plant a sunken wooden tub with a small water lily or frondose water plant such as parrot's feather (*Myriophyllum aquaticum*). Surround this with gravel, pebbles or rocks, or by small, trailing plants such as *Lysimachia nummularia* 'Aurea', and it will provide a striking focal point. If you want the sound of splashing water, a small pump will create a simple fountain or spout.

LEFT This sunken half-barrel pool, with its witty frog fountain, makes a superb focus for the corner of a town garden. The planting consists of wood millet grass (*Milium effusum*), soft shield fern (*Polystichum setiferum*), hart's-tongue fern (*Asplenium scolopendrium*) and maidenhair fern (*Adiantum capillus-veneris*).

ABOVE Here, overhanging branches have been used to create a glade-like setting within a space between trees and shrubs. The quiet, cool effect is accentuated by the broad, ribbed foliage of the hostas. The beautifully composed centerpiece contributes to the naturalistic effect with its bird-bath bowl settled firmly upon an old stump. The attractiveness of hosta flowers is often disregarded because of the beauty of the foliage but here they have a sweet-scented, misty effect.

A device as simply beautiful as a bowl or tub needs to be sited with a designer's precision to create a special atmosphere. It is no good merely dumping a container in any position in the garden and hoping it will do its stuff. You need to create a line of sight that leads to the bowl, or to plant a particular corner with interesting foliage plants, such as box or yew, ivy or ajuga, to create an appropriate setting for the bowl.

There are manufacturers and artists who specialize in making bowls and ornamental bird baths, some in making simple containers, and others on plinths for raising your bowl above ground level. You may, perhaps, find it more rewarding to make your own bowl or tub but, if you are not feeling that adventurous, it is

worth investigating local potters and even market stalls. Architectural salvage yards can be good places to search out interesting old troughs, sinks and other unusual old containers. Occasionally you may find suitable bowls and troughs for sale at garden centers. However, this does tend not to be their strongest suit, and the containers are often of inferior quality and rather fussy in style. To create a really good effect, you should look for bowls and tubs with a bold, clean shape, made of good materials with an interesting texture, such as high-quality terracotta, stoneware, real stone or wood.

It is best to use rainwater in small and shallow bowls since tap water contains a number of additives. The dissolved lime or chalk in heavily alkaline water supplies can create a series of rough rims around the inside of the bowl or tub, which are difficult to remove and may damage the bowl's glaze or fabric. If your bowl already has such a tide mark, rub it with a plastic pan scrubber, using a cleanser formulated to remove limescale, or salt and vinegar, then rinse and refill with rainwater, which is slightly acidic.

You can create a variety of effects through the careful positioning and selection of special plants for a particular situation. In a formal setting a bowl can look well on a plinth or placed next to another piece of sculpture or to plants in attractive pots – the idea is to suggest some form of interplay between them.

For a formal design, site a bowl in a corner, for instance, and create a design using taller pot plants surrounded with small pots of formal box. Arranging containers of a similar character can also produce a pleasing symmetry: a stone trough, containing clear water or water lilies, could be juxtaposed with similar troughs filled with various trailing plants or neat, starry-leaved sempervivums.

A more informal effect can be created by means of a barrel, an old laundry copper or shallow bowls. Set on a plinth or positioned on the ground, these can lead a double life both as a focal point and as a bird bath. A temporary party piece can be orchestrated by picking flowerheads and floating them on the surface of a well-designed bowl, brimming with clear water.

Barrels containing both water and water plants, arranged with others filled either with foliage plants, such as Japanese maples, grasses, sedges or bamboos, or many of the flowering shrubs make for a versatile form of garden sculpture. Gardening with containers in a small space tests your design ingenuity and by altering the position of the planted containers, and the relationships between them, you can bring variety into your small garden. Suitable plants for barrels include corkscrew rush (*Juncus effusus* 'Spiralis'), frogbit (*Hydrocharis morsus-ranae*) and hardy water lilies (*Nymphaea* 'Aurora' and *N.* 'Paul Hariot').

LEFT Bowls have been used here in conjunction with a still pool. The glazed bowls are part of a waterspill and add an extra reflectiveness to the overall design. The tender New Guinea hybrid busy lizzie (*Impatiens* New Guinea Hybrids) and the fern *Nephrolepis exaltata* join hardy Creeping Jenny (*Lysimachia nummularia*) at the water's edge, while variegated dogwood (*Cornus alba* 'Elegantissima') and golden privet (*Ligustrum ovalifolium* 'Aureum') make up the backdrop.

LEFT A study in green is simply effective: box and ivies, with a cockle-shell-shaped stone trough and a small pile of pebbles, contribute to an atmosphere of orderly reverie in this Dutch garden.

A waterproof half-barrel makes a simple and informal water container, and can be placed freestanding in grass or on gravel. Almost as simple is to excavate a hole and sink a half-barrel into a flowerbed or a small area of gravel. The barrel needs to be at least 30cm (12in) deep – half a wooden wine barrel is about the right size. This will give you enough room to accommodate some floating water plants such as *Azolla filiculoides*, a miniature water lily and a corkscrew rush (*Juncus effusus* 'Spiralis'), supported on a brick. You might also attract a few frogs if you make a platform for ease of access and egress by screwing a wooden block to the inside of the barrel from just below the normal water level to the rim. Alternatively, upend a brick against the side of the barrel, or make a "frog ladder" by building rocks up the sides.

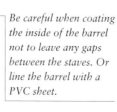

Be careful when coating the inside of the barrel not to leave any gaps between the staves. Or line the barrel with a PVC sheet.

ABOVE This freestanding water sculpture by Christine Ann Richards is made in a dark clay fired to high temperatures. The volume of water which is gently trickling in this photograph can be turned up to make a fine sheet cascading down into the bowl below. Pink argyranthemums spill from the plant container built into the upper piece and the whole effect is noiseless save for the sound of the falling water as the extra quiet pump is hidden in the base.

Most barrels on sale from garden centres come ready treated and waterproofed, but if there are leaks between the staves, pack them with clay and fill with water; as the wood swells, the barrel will become watertight. Another method is to line the barrel with a PVC sheet, or alternatively, paint them with one of the special water-proofing agents available from water garden centers. Do not use barrels or tubs previously used to hold oil, tar, wood preservatives or creosote. Make sure the barrel is thoroughly clean before putting it in place.

Plants can be inserted into the water in their basket pots or planted into a 7.5-10cm (3-4in) layer of loam-based compost. Support containers on bricks to give the required height to the plants.

The water can be brought to life by means of a small jet of water that spills into the barrel. Siting the submersible pump on the bottom of the barrel sets up a circular flow of water. An alternative arrangement could involve water spilling from one barrel to another. The pump should be situated in the lower barrel, which should be the largest one. Draw up your design first and check with a local or mail-order pool firm for advice to make sure you buy the right pump.

A planting basket confines growth, which is desirable in a small pond, but aquatics can be placed into soil on the pool bottom

Bricks can be used to adjust the planting depth for shallow water plants

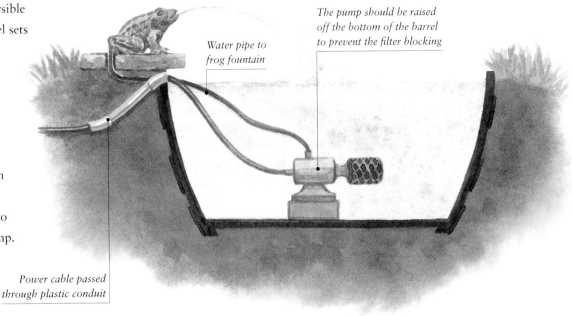

The pump should be raised off the bottom of the barrel to prevent the filter blocking

Water pipe to frog fountain

Power cable passed through plastic conduit

OPPOSITE PAGE A small rectangular stone trough, gleaming with rainwater, reflects the brilliant rudbeckias growing up through the paving. These large-flowered, low-growing *Rudbeckia fulgida* 'Goldsturm' are growing with green-flowered *Nicotiana langsdorffii* in an informal grouping, with other flowers and culinary herbs growing up through the paving.

ABOVE Some effects can be achieved only in the smallest gardens and this water-filled, metal bowl, with its soft reflections combined with the dainty surround of primulas, is a jewel. Pebbles have been arranged around the bowl, framing it informally. The primula is a late-flowering Chinese species, *Primula capitata* ssp. *sphaerocephala*, which is unusual but easily grown in moist soil.

ABOVE Stone bowls have a charm all their own that derives partly from the solidity and texture of the material from which they are made. This dark gray stone basin holds down the colorfully clashing bedding and herb plants all around it. Double poppies, orange-gold corn marigolds, fluffy orange *Inula royleana*, mauve violas and bright blue spires of *Veronica austriaca* 'Royal Blue' provide a dazzling display in the strong sunshine.

LEFT Grouping containers of water plants with soil-filled ones can make for interesting contrasts. In this relaxed paved terrace a decorated terracotta pot of verbena nudges a water barrel overspilling with plantlife: water lilies, rushes, pickerel weed (*Pontederia cordata*) and, peering from behind, a yellow Himalayan primrose (*Primula florindae*), with duckweed (*Lemna minor*) filling in the few remaining chinks of clear water.

OPPOSITE PAGE An attractive gathering of tubs and pots achieves, as a group, a balance and serenity impossible for an individual container. The soft coloration of the screens makes for an oriental flavor. The key to a good display is to vary the texture of the foliage: reed-like and spear-like leaves contrast with the flat gloss of the water lilies or the shagginess of the cyperus. This grouping is on a balcony. It is very important to make sure that the floor is adequate to support the weight when planning an arrangement such as this.

THE GARGOYLE MAN

An unusual and slightly macabre head, molded in stoneware, by the garden sculptor Dennis Fairweather, just surfaces in the duckweed-covered water, with its hands hooked over the rim in order to heave itself out of the upper barrel. A special firing process gives the finished material a verdigris effect that works well with plants, particularly foliage. A spout adds motion and the second tub makes a better splash than just a single one.

The piece is positioned in a Japanese-style arrangement with other designer bowls and stone troughs on an apron of paving that extends out on to pristine gravel. Flowers have been studiously avoided. Instead, conifers and other evergreens, ferns, and green- and purple-leaved climbing plants make a shady, mysterious background for the water- and plant-filled tubs. In the sculptor's opinion, this background sets off his work better than floral arrangements.

Each element of this tiny courtyard garden is self-contained and only the man in the double tub requires electricity and a pump, making the feature a very flexible way of building a dramatic effect using water and plants. Even the paving can be taken up and rearranged to give variety and interest to the overall design. This is a garden that can easily be transported or given a new look.

ABOVE Looking down on the double tubs gives a different impression of the swimmer. The textures and different greens of the duckweed, coniferous foliage, ferns and bamboo make for a subterranean, cave-like atmosphere.

LEFT AND OPPOSITE PAGE There is great attention to detail in the siting and finish of the tubs as well as in the head and hands. The stylized spotted bantam, also by Fairweather, at the base of the tubs picks up the color of the head. The oriental influence on this part of the garden is clearly felt in the placing of the barrels and sculpture among the evergreens: ferns, bamboo, fresh-foliaged cryptomeria and blue-gray juniper. All the plants except the barberry (*Berberis* x *ottawensis purpurea*) are in containers, so the grouping can be rearranged to bring different plants into prominence.

INFORMAL AND WILDLIFE PONDS

There are few things in life that give greater satisfaction than observing that wild flowers and wild creatures appreciate your pool almost as much as you do. Naturalistic ponds are not just the prerogative of large gardens: small pools in tiny gardens can harbor an abundance of natural life. Waterside wild flowers, such as golden marsh marigold (*Caltha palustris*), scented water mint (*Mentha aquatica*), water forget-me-not (*Myosotis scorpioides*) or brooklime (*Veronica beccabunga*) are easy to establish, as are naturalized irises. A tiny pool is capable of attracting a wide variety of pond life: showy dragonflies and damselflies, frogs, toads, water boatmen and beetles.

LEFT Colorful informality in and around an irregularly shaped pool. The delightful bog bean (*Menyanthes trifoliata*) rises above the water, while irises, hardy geraniums, primulas and royal fern grow behind them.

RIGHT This small garden has been flooded with water with a boardwalk and huge stepping stones leading away from the sociable sitting area under the festive canvas umbrella. Bamboos, small trees and shrubs on either side convey a sense of privacy and seclusion.

LEFT A pretty corner where relaxing in the chair beneath the pergola seems enormously inviting among the garden cultivars and wild plants such as flags, geum and rhododendrons, growing together in cheerful abandon.

Informal ponds look best in gardens with a relaxed, cottage-garden style. They need graded shallows for part of their periphery if you want animals to come down to drink without falling into deep water, but the rest of the banking can be quite steep, which will save on space. Another way of economizing on space and creating a semi-formal pool, which looks enticing in almost any garden, is to make the pond into a semi-circular, instead of a circular or oblong, shape. I find that this often suits the demands of a small garden better than a larger, entirely naturalistic pool.

A solid edge, made from a wooden plank, a railway tie or stone flags, creates a platform from which you can peer into the depths, while the edge of the half-moon can move from shallow water into grass or other vegetation. It is also a good idea to have a band of longer grass or clumpy plants, such as lady's mantle (*Alchemilla mollis*), irises or mint, around the edge of the pool to give wild creatures some cover.

Although wildlife ponds are usually associated with large gardens, it is the small ponds in innumerable back gardens that have become a vital resource for wildlife. Small ponds of this kind are best made from a flexible polythene or butyl liner, or from a newer, and equally strong, material known as EPDM (ethylene propylene diene monomer). These flexible liners, which are available from garden centers and water garden specialists, can be fitted exactly to the shape of your pond, and will enable you to construct shelves and shallows in the most suitable part of the garden.

An alternative to the pool-with-a-liner installation is the selection of a fiberglass pool, available ready-to-use from local nurseries and mail-order pool specialists. The shapes (the "crescent" is a favorite) and the sizes are numerous, and all you have to do is excavate a level hole that will fit the chosen pool, first placing 2½cm (1in) of sand on the bottom of the hole.

Position the wildlife pond so that you can see it from commonly used rooms, since the wildlife will keep you watching throughout the year, especially if you set up a bird table or nut bag nearby during the winter. Ensure that there is some fairly deep water in the pool (going to 1m/39in in places if you can) and you will soon find a wealth of water creatures amongst the aquatic foliage. Look out for different kinds of dragonfly and damselfly as well as frogs, toads and snails.

There are enough beautiful wild plants to make a completely natural-looking setting for the pond, but most people choose a combination of both wild and cultivated plant species that match the immediate conditions of the pond. Remember to include flowers that are attractive to bees and butterflies, such as lady's smock (*Cardamine pratensis*), meadow cranesbill (*Geranium pratense*) and other hardy geraniums and marsh marigold (*Caltha palustris*). You can also create striking plant associations using combinations of aquatic and marginal plants such as irises, water lilies, polygonums and water hyacinths.

ABOVE Poppies and red double water lilies make a brilliant contrast with the darker paving and boardwalk. The pale pink flowers of the rush-like *Butomus umbellatus* add airiness to the scene amid the irises and *Pontederia cordata*.

To create an informal pool, start by laying out a hose on the ground in the shape of the pool-to-be, and assess it from every angle, adjusting it until you are satisfied. Allow 15cm (6in) extra all round when you start to dig in order to leave room for the underlay and the liner.

Staged banking is the best option as it provides different layers for planting. Dig down to about 20-25cm (8-10in), sloping the edge slightly to the first shelf, then drop down more rapidly for the deeper area. The depth should be roughly 90cm (3ft) (plus the 15cm/6in allowance) in order to see your plants and water animals safely through the winter.

When your pool has been dug, calculate the area of liner you require by taking the maximum length of the pool and adding twice the maximum depth, then taking the maximum width and adding twice the maximum depth. Smooth the surface of the hole, pulling out any protruding stones, glass or broken china, then spread out a protective underlay of polypropylene matting or geo-textile material, which should stretch over the edge of the hole on all sides. If you have flinty soil, put down a thick layer of sand before the underlay is laid in position.

Next, lay the final liner. Smooth it roughly into place and then weigh it down. Fill the pool with water and, finally, lay the surround. To support a lawn edging, embed a stone into some mortar on the first shelf of the pool, spread a thin

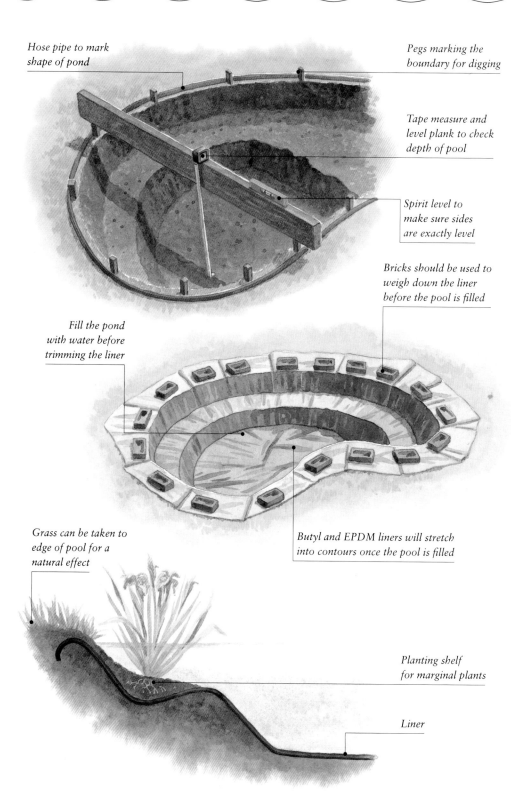

Hose pipe to mark shape of pond

Pegs marking the boundary for digging

Tape measure and level plank to check depth of pool

Spirit level to make sure sides are exactly level

Bricks should be used to weigh down the liner before the pool is filled

Fill the pond with water before trimming the liner

Butyl and EPDM liners will stretch into contours once the pool is filled

Grass can be taken to edge of pool for a natural effect

Planting shelf for marginal plants

Liner

layer of soil on top of it, then lay your turf out to the edge of the stone.

A wildlife pond is constructed in a similar manner, except that the sides should slope very gently to the water's edge, so that animals may approach without danger. It is worth putting underlay on top of the liner as well as beneath it, to give the soil and gravel something to grip and to protect the liner from solar damage. Put some soil and gravel into the base and over the shelving sides, then fill the pond, slowly trickling the water down over a square of matting or polythene. The pool will look murky at first, but it will clear in a day or so. Now gently tuck the plants (waterside ones first) into the soil, or place them in the water in their basket containers if you prefer.

ABOVE A dappled pool which emulates a pond by a woodland hedge with mind-your-own-business (*Soleirolia soleirolii*) greening the edges. An alternative would be the woodland plant, golden saxifrage (*Chrysosplenium oppositifolium*); both plants do well in shadier damper conditions where grass does not thrive. The leaves of water hawthorn (*Aponogeton distachyos*) and duckweed (*Lemna minor*) float on the dark water.

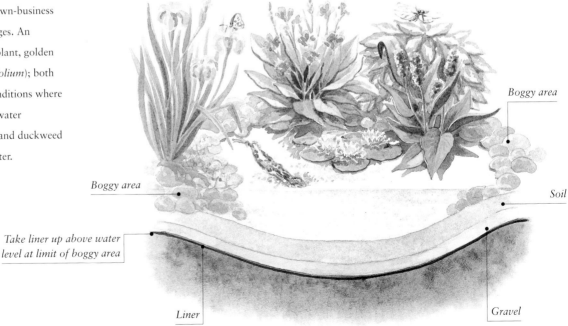

Boggy area

Boggy area

Soil

Take liner up above water level at limit of boggy area

Liner

Gravel

LEFT The pool here stretches the whole width of the small garden, with a natural wood boardwalk from the steps down to solid ground planted with conifers and other shrubs on the farthest shore. The dense bright bamboo contrasts with the copper-colored foliage beyond, and the bright new conifer foliage, the golden flags and the gold foliage of the shrubs near the fence create a lighter spot in the green composition.

RIGHT A hot-climate pool with richly colored canna lilies, golden day lilies and pink water lilies. Among the plants you can see *Pontederia cordata* with a blue flower spike, the glossy rounded leaves of *Eichhornia crassipes*, arrowhead (*Sagittaria sagittifolia*) and the blue-green crimped leaves of water lettuce (*Pistia stratiotes*). The large, umbrella-like leaves of the lotus (*Nelumbo nucifera*) precede the beautiful palest pink flowers, but it needs hot summers to flower well.

ABOVE A French interpretation of a Japanese garden with traditional stone lanterns, maples, gunnera, azaleas and the dwarf pine (*Pinus mugo*) dotted around the reflective shallow pool with its ornamental pebbles. A bleached bamboo screen, almost the same gray-white as the rock and the cobbles, creates a sense of privacy.

Cuckoo flower or
lady's smock
(*Cardamine pratensis*)

Water mint
(*Mentha aquatica*)

Water plantain
(*Alisma plantago-aquatica*)

Yellow flag
(*Iris pseudacorus*)

Marsh marigold
(*Caltha palustris*
'Multiplex')

ABOVE A pleasant pool lined informally with dog daisy (*Leucanthemum vulgare*), mimulus (*Mimulus luteus*), red campion (*Silene dioica*) and flowering rush (*Butomus umbellatus*). Beyond the water lilies is a clump of the banded rush (*Scirpus lacustris* 'Zebrinus'). It gives on to a lawn and where the pool meets the grass is a low stone edging. The floating water soldier (*Stratiotes aloides*) drifts near the white water lily.

LEFT This naturalistic pool, garlanded with wild and garden plants, looks its best in early summer as the foxgloves (*Digitalis purpurea*) and red campion (*Silene dioica*) begin to flower. There are ferns and moss growing in and around the rocks and the glowing *Euphorbia polychroma* is at its brightest next to the brightly colored *Viola tricolor*, while a dainty columbine (*Aquilegia vulgaris*) floats its purple-blue butterfly flowers above. In the pool amongst the swirls of duckweed is a fine clump of yellow flag (*Iris pseudacorus*).

RIGHT This semi-naturalistic pool graduates at the far end into a boggy area, created by making a shallow, second pool and filling it with soil so that the bog grades into the surrounding wild-flower turf. Although most of the prominent plants here are garden kinds (such as the variegated hosta and irises), mixing them with wild plants and allowing the grasses in the turf to grow and flower has created a pleasantly wild effect.

A WILDLIFE POND

This lively wildlife pond is situated at the end of a small, narrow country garden, where the ground level is 5m (16ft) above the cottage, and about 45cm (1½ft) higher than the nearby lawn. The owner of the garden, Fenella Maydew, used an existing retaining wall as a guide to water level and banked up the low side of the pool. The pond, which is roughly half-moon shaped, is lined with a thick layer of carpet to protect the butyl liner from stones, and is edged with aged limestone flags.

The bank was planted with lady's mantle (*Alchemilla mollis*), knapweed (*Centaurea nigra*) and red campion (*Silene dioica*) and has since acquired other self-sown invaders, such as the beautiful, blue-flowered meadow cranesbill (*Geranium pratense*), thus creating a haven for tiny froglets and toadlets. Yellow flag (*Iris pseudacorus*), the graceful, pink flowering rush (*Butomus umbellatus*) and marsh marigold (*Caltha palustris*), all growing in pots, were placed on shelves in the pool. Water mint (*Mentha aquatica*), eau-de-cologne mint (*Mentha* x *gracilis*) and arrowhead (*Sagittaria sagittifolia*) were planted around the muddy pond edges, while various pondweeds and duckweeds oxygenate the water. Around the pool margins, Fenella Maydew also planted meadowsweet (*Filipendula ulmaria*), lady's smock (*Cardamine pratensis*) and the

hardy, dark-flowered *Geranium phaeum*.

Every year, in late summer, the garden is cut back, to restrain vigorous species and to allow more light to reach the other plants. The pond is now a mature nine years old and the owner is very pleased with the wildlife that her informal pond has attracted into the garden.

ABOVE Looking over the wildlife pond to the border, you can see the distinct changes in level in this small garden. The existing retaining wall has been built up and lined, making a natural looking edge. From this angle we can see the water mint (*Mentha aquatica*) spreading down under the water, and the trifoliate leaves of bogbean (*Menyanthes trifoliata*) growing amongst the spear-like leaves of yellow flag (*Iris pseudacorus*).

Mixed borders

Plum tree

Raised beds

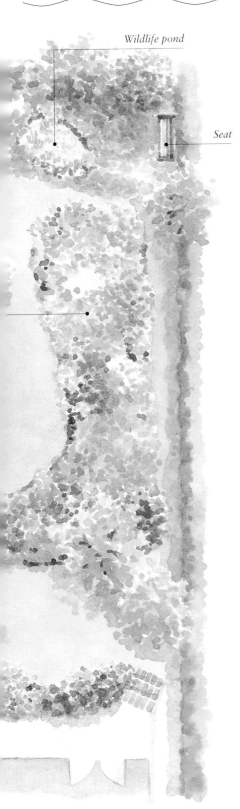

Wildlife pond

Seat

ABOVE Looking down over the foliage of elder (*Sambucus nigra*) growing under the archetypal waterside tree, the alder (*Alnus glutinosa*), across the wildlife pond to the more civilized lawns and borders with their dainty birch trees beyond. The change of level has been cleverly used to create a sense of differentiation between the two parts of the garden, although they flow naturally one into the other.

RIGHT A close-up view of this charming little pool with its informal mixture, principally of wild plants. Although the astilbe in the foreground is a garden cultivar, it fits well between its wild neighbors. Mounds of lady's mantle (*Alchemilla mollis*) cushion the far bank while tall stems of marsh marigold (*Caltha palustris*) lean towards the arrowhead (*Sagittaria sagittifolia*), just beginning to unfurl its arrow-like leaves. Red campion (*Silene dioica*), creeping buttercup (*Ranunculus repens*) and cow parsley (*Anthriscus sylvestris*) are all self seeded.

WALL-MOUNTED FOUNTAINS

Walls form a suitable backdrop as well as a practical support for bowls and fountains, enabling you to bring water into the most infinitesimal and unpromising space. You can use a simple bowl or trough, a raised pool, a pebble pool or a sunken tub in combination with your fountain. The wall also provides a point of focus whose details can be varied by adding a living surround, such as a climbing plant, or even trelliswork to frame a *trompe l'oeil* painting. By adding plants in pots and then creating a dramatic change – from a soft, lacy fern, for example, to a dramatic cordyline – you can alter the effect totally.

LEFT Water trickles from this fountain in the shape of a scallop shell, presided over by a pair of cherubs. Positioned on a shelf projecting from a wall, it juts out so the water clears the pool margin, dropping cleanly to the pool below.

ABOVE The elaborate courtyard pool with everything. The mosaic glitters against a marbled alcove, and the stone Medusa head set into it spills water into a stone basin which itself spouts over the mosaic step and into the shapely pool cleanly edged with terracotta tiles and patterned paving. Begonias, palms and balcony geraniums in pots add the final gilding.

Wall-mounted fountains fit into the tiniest of spaces, enabling people with only a minuscule back yard, alley, or squashed front garden to enjoy the sound of running water. The mechanics are simple: a small pump in a basin raises the water via a hidden hose or pipe to the fountain spout. In very small spaces, or to create a garden design with a raised focus, the fountain can be positioned 1m (39in) or so up the wall. Alternatively, a bowl or

basin can be placed on the ground in front of the wall or even in a sunken position. Whatever you choose, you will find that each option opens up a different range of possibilities for planting and design.

Well-made, and quite inexpensive, wall-mounted fountains are available as set pieces. The smallest of these all-in-one fountains can take up as little as 30 sq cm (12 sq in) but it can be more satisfying to make up your own. Visit architectural salvage yards for ideas and materials.

Wall-mounted fountains work well set into corners or as a focal point in a larger wall. If you do not have access to both sides of the wall, build a free-standing dwarf wall or an artificial stone façade, in keeping with the fabric of the house, on which you can set the fountain. A cavity wall is best for such purpose-built walls, enabling ducting and cabling to be arranged as unobtrusively as possible between the skins.

Simple planting themes work best in small spaces. The most effective plants for fountains positioned on the wall are climbing and clinging plants. Small-leaved ivy, such as the ivory-variegated *Hedera helix* 'Glacier' or pointed-leaved *H. h.* 'Sagittifolia', are easy to control in a confined space and, as evergreens, they maintain their effect during the winter. Small-flowered clematis, such as early-flowering *Clematis alpina* 'Columbine', or the *C. viticella* 'Alba Luxurians', with creamy white flowers in late summer, or

LEFT An integrated cherub wall fountain that takes up hardly any space. This one is filled with pebbles which means that its fixing has to be reinforced to take the extra weight. The most important consideration when choosing such a fountain is to make sure that the pump is quiet, or the noise can drown the sound of the water.

the dainty, sweetly scented *Rosa* 'Little Rambler', make excellent companions.

When planting around wall-mounted fountains at a lower level, try using exotic plants that benefit from the damp microclimate. Extravagantly variegated hostas and large ferns, such as the ostrich-feather fern (*Matteuccia struthiopteris*), planted with canna lilies in brilliant colors, paint bold strokes in a small garden. If you want to create a more tranquil corner plant a small-leaved hosta such as *Hosta* 'Invincible'. Ivies are invaluable, and also very good at concealing pipes. The newer astilbe hybrids, with their feathery flowers, are neat and compact, and require less boggy conditions than the larger varieties.

ABOVE This sophisticated-looking wall fountain shows what can be achieved with a little imagination. This part of the garden is shady, so the owners decided on a woodland edge planting with hellebore (*Helleborus argutifolius*), marsh marigold (*Caltha palustris*) and white-flowered sweet woodruff (*Galium odoratum*) with astilbe and clematis ready to flower later in the year. A heuchera thrives in the water.

Fountains bought from garden centers or manufacturers have a bowl in the base with a hidden pipe leading to the upper part from where it splashes down. The pipe leading from pump to spout can be hidden in three ways: either removed from view by being taken behind the wall, or left in front of the wall but concealed by planting, or recessed into the masonry.

A small pump set in the bowl recycles the water. You can buy fountain and pump as a complete unit, or purchase the sections and pump separately. If you are fitting your own pump, you will need to attach a length of pipe or hose to take the water up the wall to the point where it is connected to the spout. Try to inspect a fountain that is operating in the shop, and make sure that the pump is not a noisy one. With a small fountain, this can seriously interfere with the pleasure given by this feature, even drowning the sound of the water itself.

The essentials of installation entail bringing a power supply from an electrical plug fitted with a circuit breaker via a transformer (usually sold with the pump) to the fountain (see pp. 88-89). Site the transformer in the house, garage or shed, where it is protected from the weather, and run the cable through a pipe buried in the flowerbeds (or recessed into the wall) for concealment to the fountain.

Power cable in plastic conduit leading to a transformer

Pump and filter

Pipe partially concealed by waterline and planting

The pipework for the lion-head fountain is concealed first below the waterline and then behind planting as it rises from the submerged pump to the wall-mounted spout. The power cable is recessed into the brickwork of the fountain surround.

In this example the pipe has been taken behind the wall and emerges through the wall mask. The water spills down into a container, and then returns to the submerged tank via an overflow pipe.

The flow is adjusted simply by a control valve on the pump itself. Access is provided to the pump and control valve via a removable stone slab.

ABOVE The lion mask here has been fixed on to a decorative molding which is in turn fixed to a false wall; behind this runs the pipe that conveys the water from the basin to the spout. If there is room, this is a neat way in which to conceal pipework. Well-grown hostas whose foliage conceals their pots are just reaching the flowering stage, and *Rosa* 'New Dawn', *Clematis* 'Jackmanii' and a honeysuckle frame the fountain.

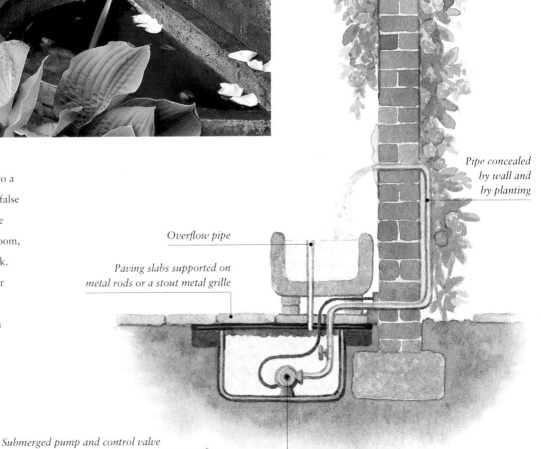

Pipe concealed by wall and by planting

Overflow pipe

Paving slabs supported on metal rods or a stout metal grille

Submerged pump and control valve

ABOVE This quasi-classical arrangement of water spouts achieves its authoritative effect through simple repetition. The water from the three pots is drained down into a joint tank and pumped into a hose with a triple diversion. The pots of bamboo echo the shape of the jars.

RIGHT This artificial stone trough, a replica of those found in Mediterranean villages, is enlivened by its unusual spout. A fair imitation of this stone has been made by adding a rough coating (composed of two parts peat to one of builder's sand and one of concrete) to an old sink which has been pre-painted with a strong impact-bonding adhesive. It soon weathers, staining and gathering algae and lichen.

ABOVE AND RIGHT Different colors and textures – the whitewashed wall, the glossy tiles in complementary shades, brick, concrete and cobble – build up the final effect in this hot corner of a courtyard. The plants are those that require hot weather and sun to thrive: palm, oleander (*Nerium oleander*) and lilies. In a nice detail the wind that blows the hair of the mask also blows the spout of water sideways.

LEFT A lion mask set into a rough stone wall spouts into a narrow reedy canal. A bright colored courtyard in red engineering bricks provides visual contrast, and a place for a terracotta pot of violas.

ABOVE A dramatic and unusual water garden dominated by a sculptural copper screen with dripping bulb-shaped containers ornamented with the smallest of green plants. The water descends into a simple formal canal that runs the width of the small garden. The flag stepping stone matches the paving beyond.

ABOVE This crocodile makes a most attractive wall spout. Plants with leathery, glossy leaves, such as bergenia and laurel, have a reflective quality that echoes the shine of the wet pebbles. They also provide a good contrast to the pendent flowers of fuchsia and the creeping stems of ivy.

THE MOSAIC FOUNTAIN

An illusion of cool serenity under a bright, unrelenting sun has been achieved in this cottage garden in Australia by creating a pleasing vista from the French doors of the house: a mosaic wall-mounted fountain on the far wall. The owner has turned a confined, narrow yard, behind his turn-of-the-century cottage, into a small paradise by complementing the shade from a mature casuarina tree with a fountain of palely gleaming, reflective tiles, and a gentle spill of water.

The quality of the materials is obviously important when the view is in close focus and an early priority was to replace ugly, green, corrugated iron fencing with gray-rendered walls in order to give an illusion of greater width. A tall, jasmine-twined archway echoes the scroll patterns of the pathway and the framed ogee-shape of the fountain. The wall-mounted fountain, which was an outstandingly successful first attempt, is constructed of broken pieces of Italian tile.

The wrought-iron table and chairs fit into either the small terrace or over the central bed, depending on where the shade is. All around the brilliant colors of poppies, impatiens, irises and mondo grass lift and soften the tranquil formality of the scene. Scent drifts over the garden from the jasmine on the arch and the low hedge of murraya that hugs the terrace.

ABOVE The water from this wall mask falls onto a shell spill and then overflows into the lower basin, which is fringed with dark green mondo grass. From here, it is pumped up to the mask via a pipe hidden behind the mosaic.

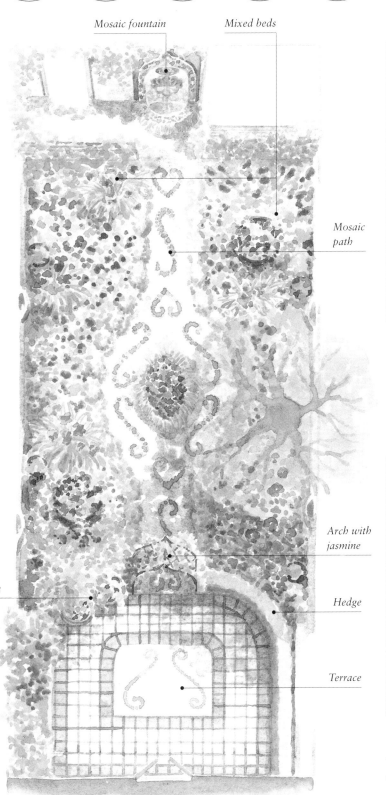

Mosaic fountain

Mixed beds

Mosaic path

Arch with jasmine

Urn

Hedge

Terrace

ABOVE From the French doors, both eye and ear are drawn over the pebble path between the flowers and leaves to the fountain on the far wall. The use of plants with leaves and flowers of differing textures contributes strongly to the overall richness of the scene.

ABOVE Looking back to the house, the shadows and well-defined shapes create a complex pattern that brings a sense of mystery to this confined garden.

CANALS, RILLS AND STEPS

Still water, once valued as highly as lively fountains, is back in fashion. The calm, formal waters that mirror ancient châteaux, the formal moats of English country houses and the rills and channels of Moorish and Spanish gardens now have their small-scale counterparts in private gardens. Exciting designs for tiny formal canals, narrow channels and other symmetrical shapes make a garden more open and inviting. A single step or a series of graduated steps, over which the water falls, adds an element of movement but the characteristic impression is of a gentle, formal calm, with the water used to bind together the design of the whole garden.

LEFT A bold design for a small area using a double pool with a single fall, a small rill and a considerable drop of over 30cm (1ft). The purple foliage and pink flowers in the planting scheme tone in well with the brick edging.

ABOVE The beauty of still water in a shallow canal to the side of an elegantly gray-painted open-arched tunnel, ornamented with wisteria and climbing roses. The roses and the velvet-leaved lady's mantle (*Alchemilla mollis*), with its bright lime-green flowers, are reflected in the dark water, broken only by the clump of *Iris sibirica* at the far end.

Still water in the form of a canal or channel can have the same kind of effect as a *trompe l'oeil* mirror in a small garden. The quality of the materials is as important as the design but this is where the small garden has the advantage for, even if you choose expensive materials, very elegant stone or marble, you will need less than for larger spaces. Stone, brick and wood, pebbles or a combination of these materials, can be fashioned into enchanting artefacts that accentuate the best characteristics of both water and materials in a small setting.

A canal that extends widthways makes a narrow garden look more expansive. Positioned alongside an alley or a flower border, it brings reflection into the design, while the addition of a fall or a gentle flow prevents stagnation. The fall can be engineered so that its small turbulence is restricted to only one part of the canal. This ensures that plants, such as water lilies, which like still conditions, can be grown in an adjacent part.

A small canal looks breathtaking, set simply into a well-kept lawn, with a focal point such as a statue, arbor or arch beyond. Two or more smaller, rectangular pools, at different levels, could be linked by a rill (a small channel or gully). On a flat surface, such as a lawn, variety can be achieved by making a series of pools of different shapes and sizes.

Rills, set into brick and stone, are most striking when used to link a pergola or terraced area with another part of the garden, concluding in a round or octagonal pool at each end. This design gives a lightness of touch to a paved or bricked courtyard where you can enjoy sitting out. Using foliage in addition to flowers prolongs the effect of the color schemes. Try purple-leaved plants such as *Heuchera micrantha* var. *diversifolia* 'Palace Purple', purple sage, and low-growing *Ajuga reptans* 'Atropurpurea', with dark, glossy, ground-hugging foliage, or scarlet, late-flowering *Dahlia* 'Bishop of Llandaff'. White or blush-pink rose and clematis cultivars are beautifully complemented by cream- or ivory-variegated shrubs, such as *Pittosporum* 'Garnettii' or *P. tenuifolium* 'Silver Queen', the elegant, white-striped grass *Phalaris arundinacea* 'Picta', or the exquisite, low-growing *Lamium maculatum* 'White Nancy', with its soft-textured leaves.

When planting, allow for variation: you can have plants in the pools and between the paving as well as small beds that echo the shapes within the design. Add or substitute plants from time to time and make a discriminating use of annuals, or tender perennials to augment summer color. Alter the arrangement of containers as plants reach their peak, moving the most striking plants to the front of the group. Then, in autumn and winter, return to the crisp formality of the original design.

ABOVE The brick internal edging to this circular pool makes a warm contrast to the stone margin, and picks up the color of the terracotta pot of variegated thyme and the herringbone path beyond. The still canal that leads into the pool is brimming with flowering plants, including the globe flower (*Trollius europaeus*) and irises.

LEFT A warm carmine carpet of primroses set off by greens: their own foliage and ferns, grass and moss. This primrose (*Primula pulverulenta*) is a native of China, where it grows in wet places and by streams. The water flows over a stone lip standing well clear of the step that supports it, making a clear bright sound.

ABOVE A complicated design where the wall fountain spills down through a circular archway to a pool that is also fed by a small rill, edged with blue engineering bricks, which takes a circular trip around the central tree and wooden chairs. The effect here, very much a designer's garden, is achieved with foliage, the gray/white of the paving and the red brick and terracotta.

There are several methods of making linked canals, rills and waterfalls. The rule, as often in small gardens, is to prefer simplicity: a semi-formal design tends to fit more easily into a small space, and bold but simple planting will make the garden seem larger.

If you want to use bricks, tiles or stone paving, it is wise to line the whole dug-out ditch with a flexible waterproof liner, before laying your bricks or paving, which you will then need to cement in place

(adding a waterproofing chemical to the mixture). Make the rill with a U-shaped profile if it is formal or has planted sides, or V-shaped if it is a simple rill running through grass, for example. For an informal effect with natural rock, take great care that the rocks are arranged with their strata running horizontally and that they tilt back slightly. A rill and pool on a small scale can be made of concrete, which must be at least 4cm (1½in) thick.

Pools can be linked by a still, narrow

canal or a sloped rill. Use any existing rise and fall in the garden to create a natural effect of spilling water. When linking pools, make sure that the upper one is smaller than the lower (in which you locate the pump), or the lower one may run out of water before the upper one begins to spill out. A naturalistic stream should have the spillway (the route the water is to take) dipping slightly at the point where you intend the water to flow, and should be wide enough to take extra flow created by a rainstorm.

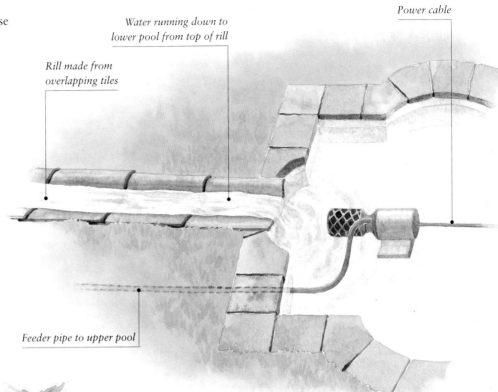

Power cable

Water running down to lower pool from top of rill

Rill made from overlapping tiles

Feeder pipe to upper pool

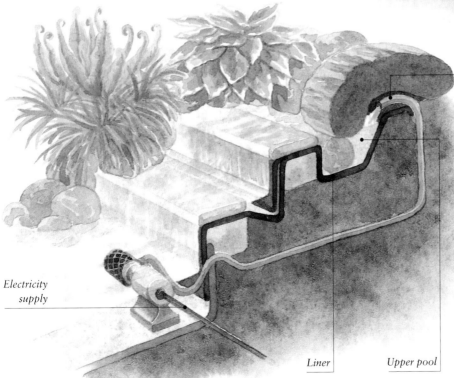

Outlet pipe

Electricity supply

Liner

Upper pool

To construct a stepped waterfall, position the concrete slabs to make the steps, then cover them with a flexible liner. Raise the liner over a slight bank at either side and disguise it with rocks and plants. Position the pump at the foot of the fall, and conceal the outlet pipe where it enters the top of the fall. If the lip of the fall stands proud of the riser of the step beneath, you will get a dramatic splash; for a gentle spill where the water curls back, make a shallow step. Experiment, and don't set anything finally into place until you are completely satisfied.

RIGHT A springtime vision of daffodils and
euphorbia in an unusual arrangement with water
pulsing down a wooden chute next to the box that
holds the euphorbia. The end of the chute extends
beyond the box and the spill is caught by the
wind. The chute is fed by water pumped through
plastic piping that passes under and behind the
box. A good early flowering euphorbia is
Euphorbia amygdaloides 'Rubra'.

ABOVE Simplicity is the rule in this elegant corner with a stepped water course falling over stone lips between ferns and curtains of glossy *Rubus tricolor*. The ferns in this warm sheltered garden are dicksonias, but in cooler places ferns such as lady fern and male fern will create this elegant effect.

RIGHT An oblong-shaped pool designed to fit the shape of the garden, with an edging of wooden planks. A tiny concrete U-profile rill flows down to this pool, which acts as a mirror to the soft-colored plants around it. These include *Erigeron karvinskianus*, bear's breeches (*Acanthus spinosus*), the white-flowered *Potentilla fruticosa* 'Abbotswood', various speedwells (*Veronica*), and *Geranium wallichianum* 'Buxton's Variety'.

LEFT A crisp design that makes good use of paving textures, with white marbled edging to the upper rectangular pool from which water flows through a little rill between flagged paving and bricks to a shallow square of water. The austere effect is softened by roses, irises and lady's mantle (*Alchemilla mollis*) in beds on the margin of the paving and by well-designed pots with blue-flowered agapanthus in them.

ABOVE An integrated design with asymmetrical still pools with a long step-spill that drops into the first L-shaped canal. The water is pumped through the system to trickle down just below the top bed. The plants in the pools are restricted to the glossy-leaved *Pontederia cordata*, which will look very smart with the box hedging when it matures.

LEFT A long stone trough makes a pretty stream bed for the water directly outside this window. The reflections of foliage and sky create chips of light that reflect the bright sun. The combined green effect of shrubs, trees and ferns is relieved by a swagged terracotta pot of pale busy lizzies (*Impatiens walleriana*). The wide edge of this raised canal doubles as a place to sit.

A TERRACOTTA RILL AND POOL

Inside this small walled garden a rill flows very gently through a decorated terracotta canal into a quiet pool. The shallow water moving over the tiled base makes lively swirls and patterns. The contrasting sounds from the four gentle falls, each of which is quite differently constructed, are audible from the jutting terrace opposite.

The tiles come from the archway of a nineteenth-century brewery that was demolished. There is stone, red brick and tiling in the adjacent barn and in the walls of the garden, so the terracotta fits well in this setting. There was no pre-set design – the owner believes that if you consider good materials that are sympathetic to their surroundings, then suitable forms will suggest themselves. Indeed, as the terracotta was unloaded and laid on the ground, the low L-shape, with its decorative fountainhead, began to take shape after only a few adjustments.

ABOVE The pump remains on the lowest setting which gives a moderate 5cm (2in) high spout of water. This rises through a pierced hole in a decorated tile, spraying over the double fall and down the gradual slope below.

LEFT Alongside the rill, various hostas, ferns, irises and ligularias create an effect that is principally dependent on the striking shapes and textures of their foliage.

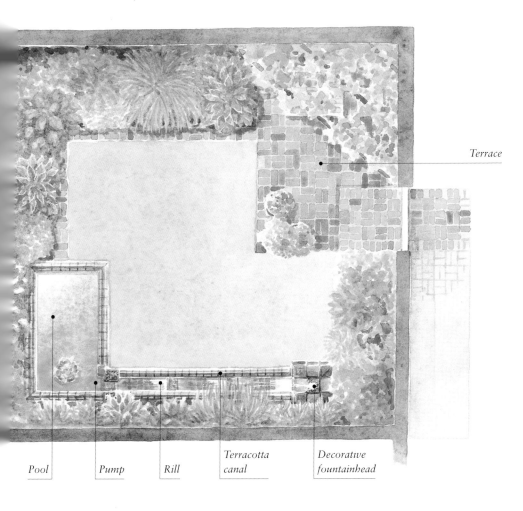

Terrace

Pool   Pump   Rill   Terracotta canal   Decorative fountainhead

ABOVE The adjacent barn makes this narrow bed rather dark, but the shade, cast by both the wall and the plants (which are all shade-tolerant), creates patterns on the surface of the water. The low-powered pump was installed in the pond, where the rill joins the pond, and quickly became concealed by algal growth. Completely silent and outstandingly reliable, it requires only a minimal cleaning of the filter from time to time. The heavy-duty return hose is laid under the narrow border between the rill and the wall.

LEFT A flexible garden structure allows for change as plants mature and your response to the garden develops. The shrubs along the west side of the pool have started to overhang the water's edge and the border is now twice its original width.

CARE AND MAINTENANCE

Provided it is well-designed, a pool or semi-natural pond, fountain or mini-falls should require only a minimum of care. The more naturalistic ponds should reach a state of dynamic equilibrium where the marginal and aquatic plants, insects, invertebrates and amphibians work together in a balanced ecosystem that needs very little interference. If you have a pump, you should make sure that the filter is clean and, towards autumn, there is the annual cutting back of plants that have grown unruly or are beginning to die back for the winter. With water as with all elements within a garden, enjoyment is the first priority; if you use your garden regularly you will notice the first sign of any problems and be able to deal with them before they get out of hand.

LEFT This pool contains a delightful muddle of flower and foliage: the pink water lily 'James Brydon' is interspersed with the yellow flowers of mimulus and green-gold lady's mantle.

FILLING THE POND

Having planned, excavated and constructed a small pond or a formal waterway, the most exciting initial step is filling it with water. If the pond is small, this is best done by filling a few buckets with water from a hose, then letting them stand overnight, or at least for a few hours, in order to de-chlorinate. When you finally pour the water into the pond, resist the temptation to do the job as rapidly as possible, and fill gently. A gentle flow of water can be achieved by trickling the water over a tile. If you have a pool with a larger capacity, use a hosepipe set to a trickle that will not disturb your carefully laid gravel or pebble edging, or disturb any compost or soil on the pool bottom.

Do not be disappointed if the water is rather murky when you have finished and your pool is brim-full; it will clear overnight as if by magic. Allow the water to rest for another day or so to rid the pool of the additives found in tap water, before you put in your waterside plants, aquatics and pondweeds, and two weeks before you add goldfish.

A gentle flow of water is achieved by flowing water over a tile, or alternatively a square of matting

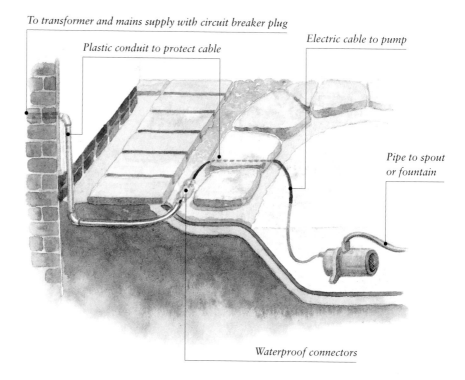

To transformer and mains supply with circuit breaker plug

Plastic conduit to protect cable

Electric cable to pump

Pipe to spout or fountain

Waterproof connectors

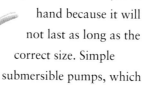

PUMPS AND FILTERS

Pump manufacturers provide tables to help you choose a pump of the right size and strength. Do not be tempted to buy a pump that is too powerful for the job in hand because it will not last as long as the correct size. Simple submersible pumps, which are cheap and readily available, are quite powerful enough for most small water gardens, although noise levels can be a consideration. Try to examine a pump in action at local flower shows or garden centers before you make your purchase; after all, you want to hear the sound of the water, not that of an electric motor. If you already have a noisy pump, consider installing it in a separate reservoir or tank rather than in the main pool. This is, in any case, a better option for a wildlife pool that has a base layer composed of loam and gravel.

Pump installation is a simple matter of laying a hosepipe from the pump to a spout, the top bowl of a cascade, or a fountain outlet. When conducting water from one part of the system to another, use a hose with the widest possible diameter (2.5cm/1in is ideal). Using ordinary hosepipe, which is generally just over 1cm (½in) in diameter, will severely strain the pump except on very short runs.

Unless you are quite used to working with electricity, it is probably better to have the electrical connections done, or at least checked, by a qualified electrician. The safest arrangement is to have a transformer positioned close to your power source, with the low-voltage cable leading to the pump sunk in the ground inside protective piping. Pumps in a pool or basin function best if they are placed on a brick or other support to help prevent detritus on the pool bottom from clogging up the filter.

As well as powering a fountain or waterfall a pump gives the hidden benefit of circulating and slightly oxygenating the water. This helps the growth of water plants and animals and prevents problems of stagnation. Some plants, such as water lilies, prefer still water, so if you wish to grow them, minimize the water flow and place the plants as far as possible from the point where the water is disturbed. A small spout or bubblejet, however, should be perfectly compatible with water lilies, even in small pools or basins.

Most pumps are economical to run – only a few pennies a day – and require minimal maintenance if they are properly sited. If you continually have breakdowns or repeatedly need to clean the filter, consider an alternative arrangement such as placing the pump in a bucket of clean water buried in the ground nearby. Simply attach a length of hose to reach from the pond to the pump. Cover the end of the hose with fine wire mesh to create a first-line filter that is simple to clean. General pump maintenance should require nothing more complicated than detaching and cleaning the filter by washing it clean of any accumulated debris.

PRUNING AND PLANT HYGIENE

In the autumn, waterside plants will begin to die back and it is a good idea to remove any dead and dying foliage before it begins to rot and contaminate the pool. Plants that are not reliably hardy, such as water chestnut, azolla, parrot's feather and tropical water lilies, should be removed from the pond and stored in an aquarium or a large bucket in a frost-free shelter during the winter. At the same time, cut out and compost rampant pondweeds. In deeper pools (about 80-100cm/32-42in), hardy plants rooted in the bottom of the pool, or established in basket-pots, can be left to overwinter.

When newly planting your pond with water lilies, it is possible to help them become established by ensuring that their planting baskets are raised up from the pool bottom on a small pile of bricks. This enables the young leaves to reach the surface almost immediately. As the water lily grows, it can be gradually lowered until it finally rests on the pool bottom.

At time of planting   *Position for basket once plant is established*

Soil

Lead weights   *Gravel or pea shingle*

KEEPING THE WATER CLEAN

In bright, sunny weather, ponds can become murky with algal growth. This usually occurs when the water warms up but the aquatic and oxygenating plants have not yet come into growth. A common sight is blanketweed, a widespread filamentous alga, which looks like long, green hair. Fortunately, in a small pond, it can be twirled like candyfloss around a forked twig and taken to the compost heap. The problem should become less serious once the established plants have begun to grow in earnest during early summer.

If your water plants are not yet mature enough, you will continue to have problems with algae. Consider introducing or increasing the quantity of duckweed or azolla, or introducing another water lily to shade the pond surface. Another solution is to take a couple of large handfuls of straw and tie them into bundles with string. Weighted down at the bottom of the pool, the degrading straw will have an effective anti-algal action. Oxygenating plants should be introduced into the pond individually as unrooted shoots, weighted with small stones or fishing weights and inserted into planting baskets or the soil on the pond bottom.

Do not clean out the pond any more than you have to. Not only does this disturb plant and animal life, but refilling the pond with nutrient-rich, chlorinated tap water can bring on a host of new problems. Even small pools and ponds, if well planted, will maintain an ecological equilibrium.

AUTUMN AND WINTER CARE

Although you might enjoy the beauty of autumn leaves floating on the surface of the water, remember to skim them off before they sink and begin to decay. For complete protection, cover small ponds and pools with wire mesh in late autumn, since the decaying leaves can impair the quality of the water. A few leaves, however, should make little difference in a deeper pool.

Pumps should be turned off during the winter months. Some manufacturers recommend disconnecting the pump altogether and keeping it under cover, but this is not usually necessary, particularly in deeper pools. Check the pump equipment thoroughly, and have parts serviced or replace them as required.

Ice on the surface of the water may be a problem in harsh winters. Water freezes slowly in layers but it rarely freezes solid, even in small pools, and so, unless you have fish (which is not desirable in very small ponds), you probably do not need to worry about taking precautions against the cold.

Peg

Wire mesh laid over pool in autumn

PLANT PROFILES

1. CREEPING, PEBBLE POOL PLANTS

Since pebble pools are more or less flush with the surface of the ground, the plants that best suit them are creeping, trailing or naturally low-growing.

Menyanthes trifoliata

❀ Bog bean (*Menyanthes trifoliata*)
A pretty bog plant with pale green three-lobed leaves and with heads of pale pink flowers in summer. It will spread attractively at the water's edge (sometimes colonizing into water 3-30cm (1-12in deep).

❀ Brooklime (*Veronica beccabunga*)
This aquatic speedwell has beautiful sky-blue flowers with a white eye that bloom from early summer, and oval darkish green leaves. Planted at the waterside, it will spread into the shallows to 8cm (3in).

❀ Creeping Jenny (*Lysimachia nummularia*)
This attractive plant comes with mid-green leaves or in a golden-leaved variety called 'Aurea'. Both do well in shade or sun and have bright yellow summer flowers.

❀ Hart's-tongue fern (*Asplenium scolopendrium*)
A shade plant of distinction that stays evergreen and produces new growth of strappy new leaves in spring, building up slowly to an attractive clump, eventually about 30cm (12in) across.

❀ Mimulus (*Mimulus guttatus*)
This species and the similar *M. luteus*, whose golden-yellow, snap-dragon like flowers are wider-mouthed and speckled rather than blotched with maroon, are naturalized in Britain. They and their many hybrids grow vigorously along the water's edge and in damp places.

❀ Soft shield fern (*Polystichum setiferum*)
A beautiful smaller fern for damp shady places with elegant well-shaped fronds. The native kind is very pretty but there are many elaborate variations.

2. AQUATIC PLANTS

Many aquatic species introduced as water garden plants have naturalized and become a problem in wild habitats. Great care should therefore be taken when disposing of any surpluses. Never throw them away carelessly or try to grow them in the wild. Composting is a good option that also benefits the garden.

❀ Floating fairy moss (*Azolla filiculoides*)
This dainty floating aquatic fern is gray-green in spring and summer, and turns coppery-red in autumn. It is hardy to only about -5°C (23°F) so it is wise to grow some indoors in a glass vase during the winter and to reintroduce it to the pond in the spring, once the water is warmer. *A. caroliniana* is hardier.

❀ Parrot's feather (*Myriophyllum aquaticum*) and whorled water milfoil (*M. verticillatum*)
Both these dainty aquatics have filigree whorls that protrude above the water level. They die back in most winters but can be overwintered in a bowl of water with a thin layer of soil on the bottom.

Myriophyllum aquaticum

Introduce individual fronds of this plant to water 10-60cm (4-24in)deep in warm weather in spring. Other myriophyllum species such as spiked water milfoil (*M. spicatum)* and milfoil have sparser whorls but they are somewhat hardier if slightly less ornamental.

❀ Pondweeds (*Elodea canadensis* and related species)

Canadian pondweed (*Elodea canadensis*), resembling a series of elongated spruce cones, grows vigorously and is a good oxygenator. Gently introduce individual fronds to the pond in spring. It will grow happily in sun or shade in water 10cm-1m (4-39in) deep and survive hard winters by producing special buds that lie dormant in the bottom of the pond. Similar pondweeds such as *Lagarosiphon major* (syn. *Elodea crispa*) and *E. densa* and other species are also good oxygenators.

❀ Common duckweed (*Lemna minor*)

This floating weed will rapidly spread and cover a still pool. This can sometimes be an advantage, particularly in the spring when the bright sun, falling on a clear pool, prompts algae into an unwelcome spurt of murky growth. The duckweed will shade the pool until the aquatic water plants have begun to grow strongly (it is much valued in the bright sun of California for this reason). As spring advances, the duckweed can be easily removed with no ill effect. Common duckweed has the familiar small flat green leaf-like fronds; ivy-leafed duckweed (*Lemna trisulca*) is starry in shape and floats a little below the surface. Introduce duckweeds to fairly still water at any time except winter.

❀ Hornwort (*Ceratophyllum demersum*)

This excellent oxygenating, delicately fronded plant is hardy down to about -15°C (5°F). Introduce young plants at any time except winter. Propagate by breaking off small pieces and allow them to float free.

❀ New Zealand pygmyweed (*Crassula helmsii*)

A long-stemmed plant with small, narrow leaves and tiny, pinkish white flowers. Naturalized in Britain, it is spreading rapidly. To introduce it, tuck pieces into the mud at the bottom of the water 25-95cm (10-38in) deep in warm weather.

❀ Water hawthorn (*Aponogeton distachyos*)

An attractive plant with floating, oval leaves and white, scented flowers in late spring and autumn. It is sporadically naturalized in southern Britain. In mild climates, such as in zones 10-11, it remains evergreen in winter. Elsewhere, plant tubers or plants in spring, in a basket or into the bottom mud in water 25-60cm (10-24in) deep for temporary pleasure.

❀ Water soldier (*Stratiotes aloides*)

A hardy perennial with rosettes of spiky leaves, rather like the tops of pineapples, and small white- or pink-tinged flowers in summer. The plant floats partly submerged on the pond surface and sinks to the bottom in winter. Place young plants in water at least 30cm (12in) deep in spring.

3. WATER LILIES FOR SMALL CONTAINERS, TUBS AND VERY SHALLOW POOLS

These hardy small water lilies with a limited spread should be planted so that there is 15cm (6in) of water above the soil level. Plant in late May or June. Anticipate a surface spread of 20-30cm (8-12in).

❀ *Nymphaea* 'Helvola Pygmy'

Starry, yellow flowers and small foliage

❀ *Nymphaea* 'Joanne Pring'

Deep pink flowers, compact growth

❀ *Nymphaea* 'Pygmaea Rubra'

Nymphaea alba

Slightly larger both in foliage and flowers, which turn from pink to dark red.

❀ *Nymphaea* 'Albatross'

White-flowered, dwarf enough for tubs.

4. SMALL WATER LILIES

These hardy water lilies can be planted in spring in soil at the bottom of larger pools or kept in a basket. The rough guides to planting depths given below refer to the water depth above the soil level of the plant (not counting roots and pot or soil depth). Unlike tropical water lilies, only winter hardy in zones 10-11, these hardy water lilies become permanent pool plants.

❀ *Nymphaea* 'Froebelii'
Crimson, free-flowering with neat leaves.
Planting depth: 15-17cm (6-7in)

❀ *Nymphaea* 'Graziella'
Golden-orange flowers, 5-8cm (2-3in)
across. Planting depth: 15-40cm (6-16in)

❀ *Nymphaea* 'Indiana'
For slightly larger ponds, flowers are
peach turning to red, with purple marked
leaves. Planting depth: approximately 25-
45cm (10-18in)

❀ *Nymphaea* 'James Brydon'
Reliable, all-purpose water lily with large
pink flowers and rounded leaves, which
can adapt to most sizes of pool. Planting
depth: 15-45cm (6-18in)

❀ *Nymphaea* 'Laydekeri Lilacea'

Nymphaea 'Laydekeri
Lilacea'

Compact, pale mauve free-flowering.
Planting depth: 12-30cm (5-12in)

❀ *Nymphaea* 'Odorata Minor'
White, scented flowers.
Planting depth: 12-30cm (5-12in)

5. WATERSIDE PLANTS

Waterside or marginal plants make a tiara
of flower and foliage that contributes

hugely to the overall beauty of a pond.
They are planted in the autumn or spring.

❀ Arum lily (*Zantedeschia aethiopica*)
Large white flowers 4in (10cm) across.

❀ Astilbe (*Astilbe*)
Suitable compact hybrids include *A.*
'Fanal' (red), *A.* 'Intermezzo' (peachy-
salmon), *A.* 'Maintz' (lilac pink), *A.*
'Bronce Elegans' and *A.* 'Dunkellachs'
(both dark salmon) and *A.* 'Rosea' (pink).

❀ Hosta (*Hosta*)
Though usually thought of as foliage plants,
hostas also have attractive lilac or white
flowers. Try the white-variegated *H.*
crispula for sunnier places, the tough *H.*
'Invincible' if you are bothered by slugs, *H.*
fortunei var. *albopicta*, which has golden-
centered foliage, or *H.* 'Albomarginata',
which has smudged white margins.

❀ Iris (*Iris laevigata* and *I. sibirica*
hybrids)
I. sibirica is a beautiful small-flowered iris
with narrow green leaves and many
differently colored cultivars. *I. laevigata*
'Variegata' is particularly beautiful with
elegant cream-striped leaves and blue-
purple flowers.

❀ Lady's smock (*Cardamine pratensis*)
A small plant, 20cm (8in) tall, with
attractive silvery-pink four-petalled
flowers, which bloom in early spring. A
double form is equally attractive. It is the
food plant of the orange tip butterfly.

❀ Marsh marigold (*Caltha palustris*)
A lovely springtime plant, 25cm (10in)
high with glorious golden cups that show

up well against the dark green heart-
shaped leaves. There is a double form *C.p.*
'Multiplex' which is smaller and more
compact.

❀ Flowering rush (*Butomus umbellatus*)

Butomus umbellatus

A deciduous rush-like plant 1m (39in)
high with narrow leaves and pink to
reddish flowers in the summer.

❀ Snake's-head fritillary (*Fritillaria
meleagris*)
Dainty, checkered, cowbell-shaped flowers
in deep pink hang from a 25-30cm (10-
12in) stem which is gray-green like the
grass-like leaves. There is also a white
form available, *F. m. alba*.

❀ Sweet flag (*Acorus calamus*
'Variegatus')
The variegated cultivar of this iris-like
plant has gold and creamy striped leaves.
Eventually it forms a clump about 1m
(39in) or a little less in height. The flowers
are like elongated green cones.

❀ Water mint (*Mentha aquatica*)
This waterside plant is very vigorous but
can be mown or pulled out easily. It looks
and smells rather like spearmint, but is
shorter, about 25-30cm (10-12in) high.

INDEX

Acknowledgments

1 Sue Atkinson/Reed International Books Ltd (Designer: Myles Challis); 3 Corbis/Michael Boys Collection; 5 Anthony Paul/The Garden Picture Library; 6-7 Steven Wooster/The Garden Picture Library (Designer: Anthony Noel); 8 John Glover/The Garden Picture Library; 9 Noel Kavanagh (Designer: Angela Kirby); 10-11 Clive Nichols (Contractor: Cecil Bicknell); 12-13 N. & P. Mioulane/Mise au Point; 14 Jerry Harpur (Designer: Jim Matsuo, Los Angeles, California); 15 Clive Nichols (Designer: Jill Billington); 16 Clive Nichols (Dales Stone Company); 18 left Marianne Majerus; 18 right Andrew Lawson (Sue Whittington, London); 19 Georges Lévêque (Mr & Mrs Camus, Chéchy, France); 20 John Glover/The Garden Picture Library; 21 left Beatrice Pichon (Designer: Guy Laine); 21 right Gary Rogers; 22-23 above Marianne Majerus; 23 below Clive Nichols (The Crossing House, Cambs.); 24-25 Derek St. Romaine; 26 Neil Campbell-Sharp (Designer: Dan Pearson); 27 above Jerry Harpur (Designer: Simon Fraser, Hampton, Middlesex); 27 below Jerry Harpur (Designer: Mark Rummary, Suffolk); 29 Brigitte Thomas; 30 left Jerry Harpur (Designer: Jane Fearnley-Whittingstall, Wootton-under-Edge, Gloucestershire); 30-31 Derek Fell; 31 right Photograph courtesy of Australian House & Garden magazine; photography by Robert Karri-Davies; 32 Arnaud Descat/ Mise au Point (Designer: E. le Hardy; Owner: M. Della France); 33 Noel Kavanagh (Designer: Angela Kirby); 34 left Jerry Harpur (Designer: Jean Melville-Clark, Long Melford, Suffolk); 34-35 Jane Legate/The Garden Picture Library; 35 right John Glover/The Garden Picture Library; 36-37 Photography by Eric Victor (Designer: Philip O'Malley); 38-39 Clive Nichols (frog by Stiffkey Lamp Shop); 40 Garden Matters; 41 above Frederic Marre/Mise au Point; 41 below Marijke Heuff (Mr & Mrs Voute-Droste); 42 Neil Campbell-Sharp (Barters Farm); 44 Clive Nichols (Red Gables, Worcestershire) ; 45 left Marijke Heuff (Mrs L. Goossenaerts-Miedema); 45 right Andrew Lawson (Herterton House, Northumberland); 46 Arnaud Descat/Mise au Point; 47 above Annette Schreiner ; 48-49 Derek St. Romaine (Designer: Dennis Fairweather); 50-51 Neil Campbell-Sharp (Tin Penny); 52 left Beatrice Pichon (Designer: Guy Laine); 52 right Gary Rogers; 53 Gary Rogers/The Garden Picture Library ; 55 John Miller; 56 left Clive Nichols (Designer: Richard Coward); 56 right Derek Fell; 57 Georges Lévêque (Landscape Designer: M.François Bonnin, St.Nexans, France); 58 Photos Horticulture; 59 above John Glover (Gavin Landscape Design); 59 below Heather Angel; 60-61 Andrew Lawson (Fenella Maydew, Daglingworth, Glos.); 62-63 Mick Hales; 64 Tim Street-Porter (Whitley House, California); 65 left Clive Nichols (Longacre, Kent); 65 right Jerry Harpur (Dr & Mrs Parris, Bury St. Edmunds, Suffolk); 67 Derek St. Romaine; 68 Derek Fell (Fountain design: Cevan Forristt); 69 above Ron Sutherland/The Garden Picture Library; 69 left Marianne Majerus (Designers: Duane Paul); 69 below right Marianne Majerus; 70-71 Derek St. Romaine (Designer: Cleve West; Sculptor: Johnny Woodford); 70 left Gary Rogers; 71 right Neil Campbell-Sharp (Geoffrey Smith); 72-73 Photographs courtesy of Australian House & Garden magazine; photography by Tim Griffith (Designer: Philip O'Malley); 74-75 Gary Rogers; 76 Steven Wooster/The Garden Picture Library; 77 above Eric Crichton; 77 below John Glover; 78 Designer: Richard Baxter of Brambles Garden Landscapes (Mr and Mrs Webster); 80 Jerry Harpur (Designer: Jean Hawkswell, Surrey); 81 Georges Lévêque (Trebah, Cornwall); 82 left Brigitte Thomas; 82 right Annette Schreiner; 83 right Ron Sutherland/ The Garden Picture Library; 83 left Tim Street-Porter (Robert Evans); 84-85 Clive Nichols (Designer: Kim Wilkie); 86 Georges Lévêque.